The Book of the
VIVA HC and MAGNUM

Three popular Viva saloons: *top*, the two-door SL (1800 shown here); *centre*, the 2300 SL, with Rostyle wheels; *bottom*, the four-door SL

The Pitman Motorists' Library

The Book of the
VIVA HC
and MAGNUM

Servicing and Maintenance in the Home Garage
Covering the 1,159 c.c., "90," 1,256 c.c., 1600,
1800, and 2300 models.

Staton Abbey, M.I.M.I.

Pitman Publishing

First published 1974

SIR ISAAC PITMAN AND SONS LTD
Pitman House, Parker Street, Kingsway, London WC2B 5PB
PO Box 46038, Banda Street, Nairobi, Kenya
SIR ISAAC PITMAN (AUST.) PTY LTD
Pitman House, 158 Bouverie Street, Carlton, Victoria 3053, Australia
PITMAN PUBLISHING CORPORATION
6 East 43rd Street, New York, NY 10017, USA
SIR ISAAC PITMAN (CANADA) LTD
495 Wellington Street West, Toronto 135, Canada
THE COPP CLARK PUBLISHING COMPANY
517 Wellington Street West, Toronto 135, Canada

ISBN 0 273 00228 7

Text set in 8/9 pt. Monotype Times New Roman, printed by photolithography,
and bound in Great Britain at The Pitman Press, Bath
G. 4306:19

How this book was planned

WHETHER from choice or because of high garage labour charges, more and more owners are turning to do-it-yourself maintenance nowadays, and one of the objects of this book is to make the initiation of the novice as painless as possible.

For the more experienced owner, jobs such as ignition timing, carburettor servicing and adjustment, brake relining and similar work that is mostly outside the scope of the ordinary instruction book, are fully covered.

To help the beginner and expert alike to tackle this sort of work more confidently, the jobs have been broken down into easy, logical steps, using modern "programmed instruction" techniques:

Information: the reasons for doing the work, and an outline of the basic theory in non-technical terms.

Operation: the bare bones of the job, briefly described in simple step-by-step form (often this will be all that the expert requires).

Explanation: supplementary notes on how to do the work, including practical tips for the beginner and whether special service tools will be needed.

Anyone who intends to carry out major overhauls (which are beyond the scope of this book) will be glad to know that Service Training Manuals for the Viva and Magnum are available from Vauxhall dealers or from the Service Department, Vauxhall Motors Ltd., Luton, Beds, LU2 0SY. Grateful thanks are due to Vauxhall Motors for permission to reproduce some of the illustrations from these manuals.

Every care has been taken to check the information given in this book, but no responsibility can be taken for mistakes, or for subsequent changes in the specifications of the models covered.

Creek House   STATON ABBEY
St. Osyth
Essex

The Viva estate is a handsome car, with a widely-opening tailgate giving access to a flat loading platform and a large goods-carrying space

The top-power version of the Viva estate cars, the 2300 model, combines the generous space with a lively performance from its twin-carburettor engine. The Magnum 2300 estate is very similar

Contents

1 Getting to know your car

Practical owners usually like to browse through facts and figures, and in any case much of the information given in the following pages will be needed during routine servicing.

Useful as these tables are, however, there is one point to bear in mind: car design is never static and modifications are often made during the production run of a particular model, which may affect some of the figures in the tables. If in doubt, you will usually find your Vauxhall dealer ready to give friendly advice.

ENGINE MAINTENANCE DETAILS

Valve clearances, hot

Viva "90," 1,256 c.c.	
Inlet and exhaust	0·008 in. (0·20 mm)
Viva 1,159 c.c., inlet	0·006 in. (0·152 mm)
exhaust	0·010 in. (0·254 mm)
All other models, inlet	0·007–0·010 in. (0·18–0·25 mm)
exhaust	0·015–0·018 in. (0·38–0·46 mm)

Sparking plug type, normal running

Viva 1,159 c.c., "90," 1,256 c.c.	AC 42XLS
Viva 1600	AC 42TS
(To cure plug overheating)	AC 41T
Viva and Magnum 1800	AC R41TS
Viva and Magnum 2300	AC R42TS

Sparking-plug gap, all models   0·030 in. (0·75 mm)

Ignition distributor contact-breaker gap   0·020 in. (0·50 mm)

Ignition timing

Viva 1,159 c.c., 1,256 c.c.	$4\frac{1}{2}°$ B.T.D.C.
All other models	9° B.T.D.C.

Oil pressure, hot (at 3,000 r.p.m.)

Viva 1,159 c.c. and "90"	35–45 lb/sq in. (2·5–3·2 kg/cm^2)
All other models	45–55 lb/sq in. (3·2–3·9 kg/cm^2)

ENGINE SPECIFICATION

	Bore	Stroke	Capacity	Brake Horse Power (DIN) b.h.p. at r.p.m.	
Viva 1,159 c.c.	. 77·7 mm (3·062 in.)	60·9 mm (2·40 in.)	1,159 c.c. (70·7 cu in.)	49	5,300
Viva "90" .	. 77·7 mm (3·062 in.)	60·9 mm (2·40 in.)	1,159 c.c. (70·7 cu in.)	62	5,500
Viva 1,256 c.c..	. 80·98 mm (3·188 in.)	60·96 mm (2·40 in.)	1,256 c.c. (76·6 cu in.)	52·8*	5,200
Viva 1600 .	. 85·7 mm (3·375 in.)	69·2 mm (2·276 in.)	1,599 c.c. (97·5 cu in.)	70	5,100
Viva and Magnum 1800 . .	. 85·7 mm (3·375 in.)	76·2 mm (3·00 in.)	1,759 c.c. (107·4 cu in.)	77	5,200
Viva and Magnum 2300 . .	. 97·54 mm (3·840 in.)	76·2 mm (3·00 in.)	2,279 c.c. (139·0 cu in.)	110	5,200

Number of cylinders, all models   .   .   . 4

Firing order, all models   .   .   . 1, 3, 4, 2

Standard compression ratio
Viva "90" . . . . . : . 9·0 : 1
Viva 1,256 c.c. (from September 1973) : : . 9·2 : 1
All other models . . . . . . 8·5 : 1

* From September 1973, 58·5 b.h.p.

CAPACITIES (approx.)

	Imp gal	Litres
Fuel tank		
Viva 1,159 c.c., "90," 1,256 c.c., 1600	8	36·4
Viva and Magnum 1800, 2300	12	54·6
	Imp pints	*Litres*
Cooling system (add 1 pint for heater)		
Viva 1,159 c.c., "90," 1,256 c.c.	9¼	5·3
Viva and Magnum 1600, 1800, 2300	13	7·4
Engine sump refill (with filter change)		
Viva 1,159 c.c., "90," 1,256 c.c.	5	2·8
Viva and Magnum 1600, 1800, 2300	8	4·5
***Gearbox**		
Viva 1,159 c.c., "90," 1,256 c.c.	0·9	0·5
Viva and Magnum 1600, 1800, 2300	2¼	1·4
Rear axle		
Viva 1,159 c.c., "90," 1,256 c.c., 1600	1¼	0·7
Viva and Magnum 1800, 2300	2½	1·4

* When automatic transmission is fitted, fluid should be changed every 24,000 miles, combined with service and adjustment. This is a job for a Vauxhall dealer.

COOLING SYSTEM

Type	. Pressurized, pump circulation, thermostatically controlled
Filler-cap Pressure	. 15 lb/sq in. (1·1 kg/cm^2)
Thermostat opening temperature	
Western Thomson	. 88°C (190°F)
AC	. 82°C (180°F)

FUEL SYSTEM

	Synchromesh Gearbox models	Automatic Transmission models
Fuel grade—all models with standard compression ratio	. 97–98 octane (4-star in UK)	
Fuel pump type . . .	. AC mechanical	
Carburettor	*Synchromesh Gearbox models*	*Automatic Transmission models*
Viva 1,159 c.c. . . .	. Zenith 30IZ	—
Viva "90"	. Zenith/Stromberg 150CDS	Zenith/Stromberg 150CDST
Viva 1600, 1800 . . .	. Zenith 36IV	Zenith 36IVT
Viva 2300	. Twin Zenith/Stromberg 175CD-2S	Twin Zenith/Stromberg 175CD-2ST
Viva 1,256 c.c. . . .	. Zenith 30IZ (or Stromberg 150CDSEV)	Zenith 34IVET
Magnum 1800 . . .	. Zenith 36IVE	Zenith 36IVE
Magnum 2300 . . .	. Twin Zenith/Stromberg 175CD2SE	Twin Zenith/Stromberg 175CD2SET

RECOMMENDED LUBRICANTS AND FLUIDS (Temperate climates)

Engine	. Multigrade oil 20W/50 or 10W/40
Ignition distributor shaft, contact-breaker pivot, automatic timing control	. Engine oil
Carburettor damper . .	. 20W/50 engine oil
Gearbox and rear axle .	. SAE 90EP or 90/140EP gear oil
Automatic transmission .	. Automatic Transmission Fluid supplied by Vauxhall dealer
Front-wheel hub bearings . .	. Multipurpose grease
Brake master cylinder . .	. Castrol-Girling Brake Fluid (Green)
Grease gun	. Multipurpose grease with molybdenum disulphide (Moly)

DIMENSIONS AND WEIGHTS (approx.)

Length	13 ft 7 in. (4·140 m)
Width	5 ft 4¾ in. (1·645 m)
Height	4 ft 5½ in. (1·359 m)
Ground clearance	5 in. (127 mm)
Weight	
Viva 1,159 c.c. and 1,256 c.c. saloons . .	16½ cwt (838 kg)
Viva and Magnum 1800 and 2300 saloons . .	18½ cwt (940 kg)
Estate cars	Approx. ½ cwt (25 kg) heavier

STEERING

Type . . .	Rack-and-pinion steering gear with flexible couple and collapsible column, and steering/ignition lock
Front-wheel alignment .	0·045 in. (1·2 mm) toe-out to 0·045 in. (1·2 mm) toe-in

The steering geometry and front-wheel alignment can be checked only with special gauges.

ELECTRICAL SYSTEM

Type . . .	12 volt, negative earth, with alternator

TORQUE WRENCH SETTINGS

As emphasized in other chapters, it is advisable to tighten some of the more important nuts and bolts to a specified torque figure, expressed in lb ft (kg m), in order to obtain the correct tightness without risking over-stressing a bolt or a stud or distorting a part. Torque-wrench figures which will be needed when carrying out the jobs described in this book are given below.

	Condition (see below)	Tightening Torque lb ft	kg m
Push-rod Engines			
Connecting-rod bolts	1	25	3·46
Crankshaft main bearing bolts . . .	1	58	8·02
Flywheel and flexplate bolts . . .	3	25	3·46
Cylinder-head bolts	2	49	6·77
Oil filter bolt	2	14	1·94
Sparking plugs	2	25	3·46
Overhead-camshaft Engines			
Connecting-rod bolts . . .	1	47	6·50
Crankshaft main bearing bolts . . .	1	83	11·48
Flywheel bolts	2	48	6·64
Cylinder-head bolts	2	83	11·48
Camshaft housing bolts . . .	2	15	2·07
Sparking plugs	2	15	2·07
Brakes and Wheels			
Wheel nuts	2	51	7·05
Calliper to steering knuckle bolts . .	2	33	4·56
Disc to hub	4	18	2·49
Rear brake flange plate nuts . .	2	13	1·80

1 Oiled threads   **2** Clean dry threads   **3** Sealed threads   **4** Loctite applied

TYRES

The pressures given below are average figures only. The latest recommendations by the manufacturers of the tyres fitted to your car should always be checked, as there are sometimes variations between different makes. Most garages and tyre specialists should have this information.

Tyre size	Pressures lb/sq in. (kg cm^2)		
	Normal running Front and rear	Fully loaded Front	Rear
5·20–13 saloons	24 (1·69)	30 (2·11)	30 (2·11)
5·20–13 estate cars	22 (1·55)	24 (1·69)	30 (2·11)
6·2S–13 saloons	22·(1·55)	22 (1·55)	26 (1·83)
6·2S–13 estate cars	22 (1·55)	24 (1·69)	30 (2·11)
5·60–13 4-ply rating	24 (1·69)	30 (2·11)	30 (2·11)
5·60–13 6-ply rating	24 (1·69)	35 (2·32)	35 (2·32)
155 SR–13 radial-ply	24 (1·69)	30 (2·11)	30 (2·11)
175/70 HR–13 radial-ply	24 (1·69)	28 (1·97)	28 (1·97)

For continuous high-speed cruising, raise the normal front and rear pressures by 4 lb/sq in. (0·28 kg/cm^2)

2 Servicing for beginners

So you have a practical turn of mind, and would like to carry out as much routine maintenance and servicing of your car as possible? One must draw the line somewhere, of course, and the sort of jobs that you should tackle will depend on your experience and on the tools and equipment at your disposal. Routine adjustments and servicing should be well within your scope, even if you are a novice. As you gain experience, you should be able to cope with the more advanced work described in this book.

The cost of a basic tool kit will eventually be more than offset by savings in garage labour charges, which usually form the largest part of servicing and repair bills nowadays; but a bigger dividend is the knowledge that no items have been scamped or overlooked. There is a good chance, too, of discovering any trouble at an early stage, before it can result in an expensive repair or a roadside breakdown.

The Tools You Will Need. No job can be done properly without the right tools. You will probably have to buy a few items to supplement the collection of screwdrivers, pliers and so forth that the average home handyman accumulates over a period of years.

"Unified" screw threads are extensively used on these cars and nuts and bolts of this type call for the use of American spanner sizes (usually termed S.A.E. or A/F spanners). If you have a legacy of Whitworth spanners from an earlier car, don't be tempted to use them on Unified nuts. They may appear to be a reasonably good fit, but there is a risk of damaging the corners of the hexagons if any stress is applied.

If would be advisable to purchase a set of good-quality ring or socket spanners in a range of sizes from $\frac{1}{4}$ in. to $\frac{9}{16}$ in., to supplement the open-jawed spanners. If you can afford an extension drive and, possibly, a ratchet handle, so much the better.

Items such as a torque-indicating wrench, a vacuum gauge and an engine compression gauge are desirable (a torque wrench is a "must" if you do any overhauls or repairs), but these can wait until you are ready to tackle more ambitious work.

There is no need to pay top prices for tools which will be used only occasionally in the home garage, but avoid very cheap tool sets which are simply marked "Foreign." These are usually of very poor quality and have a short life. Tools from West Germany, however, are normally very good value for money.

BASIC TOOL KIT

The following are essential items for routine servicing, which can be added to as more ambitious work is undertaken. Special service tools (when needed—and fortunately this does not apply to most of the jobs covered by this book) can sometimes be hired from a local Vauxhall dealer:

Set of open-ended or ring, or combination spanners, A/F sizes $\frac{1}{4}$–$\frac{9}{16}$ in.
Set of socket spanners, with extension, in same size range
Selection of screwdrivers, including two sizes for cross-head screws
Large and small adjustable spanner
Self-locking adjustable spanner (Mole wrench type)
Side-cutting and pointed-nose 6 in. pliers
Set of feeler gauges
Sparking plug gap-setting tool
Tyre-pressure gauge
Tyre tread-depth gauge
Engineer's hammer (ball pane)
Fine carborundum stone
Wire brush
Inspection lamp

A good tyre-pressure gauge is essential. Garage pressure gauges are not always as accurate as they should be; and pressures should always be checked with the tyres *cold*, which is obviously impossible if the car has to be driven to a garage or if pressures are checked during the course of a journey. Take a tip from rally and competition drivers and spend a little more on a dial-type gauge, which gives clearer readings than the telescopic type.

A tyre tread-depth gauge is an inexpensive item which will enable you to keep a check on the rate of wear of the tyres and will also indicate when they are due for replacement. The official regulation in Britain calls for 1 mm of tread over three quarters of the width of the tread pattern, around the complete circumference of the tyre, but it is much safer to change the tyres when the treads are worn down to a depth of 2 mm.

An electrical drill is, perhaps, something of a luxury, but the way in which it can speed-up a surprisingly large number of jobs, particularly if it is provided with the usual range of accessories, such as wire brushes for decarbonizing the cylinder head, a grindstone and a lambswool polishing mop, renders it a real worthwhile investment for an owner who carries out any appreciable amount of work.

Turning the Engine when Making Adjustments. The fact that modern engines are not provided with starting handles makes it difficult to rotate the crankshaft while setting the valve clearances, adjusting the gap between the contact-breaker points or checking the ignition timing.

The most usual way of turning the engine when a manual gearbox is fitted is to remove the sparking plugs (in order to relieve the compression in the cylinders and allow the engine to turn easily), engage top gear and then push the car backwards or forwards.

If the car has an automatic transmission, of course, this method is ruled out and you will probably have to resort to using a spanner on the crankshaft pulley nut at the front of the engine. Some garage mechanics become adept at turning the engine by operating the starter motor for a few seconds at a time, but this method is only justifiable as a time-saver to obtain approximately the correct position of the flywheel. Final adjustment must be made by one of the methods just described, since accuracy is essential when setting the ignition timing, or adjusting the valve clearances.

Don't be tempted to pull on the fan blades.

Workbench and Storage. A workbench will be needed for any jobs that are done on components that have been removed from the car, but it is quite possible to make do with a stout kitchen table, which can often be picked up for a few pence at an auction. If any but elementary servicing is carried out, a vice will be needed. This can often be obtained quite cheaply from a shop which deals in Ministry surplus equipment.

It is much more economical to purchase oil in bulk—say in gallon rather than in pint or quart tins—and a five-gallon drum works out even more cheaply. A wooden stand can be made up to take the drum and a draw-off tap can be purchased to replace the screwed plug in the side of the drum. Needless to say, when fitting the tap the drum should be laid on its side, with the screwed plug uppermost.

Working Beneath the Car. If an inspection pit is not available, a pair of drive-on wheel ramps will also be needed. A cheaper alternative is a pair of adjustable axle stands. These have the advantage of leaving the wheel free to rotate. On the other hand, it takes only a minute or two to drive the front or rear wheels on to a pair of ramps, whereas both sides of the car must be jacked-up to allow stands to be placed below the jacking points. For further notes on jacking, *see* page 88.

For obvious reasons, ramps or axle-stands which lift only one end of the car must not be used when checking the oil-levels.

Finally, never be tempted to work beneath the car when it is supported only by the jack or by an insecure pile of bricks.

3 Planning do-it-yourself maintenance

THE home-servicing scheme outlined on pages 11–13 broadly follows the latest Euroservice 365 times-and-mileage scheme operated by Vauxhall dealers. The A, B and C services described in the car instruction book are covered (plus the intermediate safety checks), but some additional jobs that are within the scope of the practical owner have been included. Also, if you have a new car, it is advisable to carry out a 6,000-miles check after the first 3,000 miles have been covered, and then follow the normal schedule. If you have bought a used car, give it a 12,000-miles check immediately, to make sure that all is well. Some car dealers do this as a matter of course during pre-sale preparation of used cars.

Each item in the home-maintenance schedule has been given a job number, the first part of which indicates the frequency with which the work must be done: W-1 is a weekly job, 6-1 a 6,000-mile service item, and so on. On turning to the page reference, you will find a detailed explanation of the job.

If you carry out maintenance single-handed at home, however, you will quickly discover that the main drawback of a rigid schedule is the time factor. The 6,000-mile or 12,000-mile service, for example, is likely to take up the better part of a week-end. There is a lot to be said, therefore, for spreading the load as much as possible.

Draw up a maintenance chart which will allow two or three jobs to be done comfortably in an hour or so once a week. How this is arranged will depend, of course, on the average weekly mileage.

There is no need to adhere too rigidly to the specified mileage intervals. A few hundred miles on either side are not critical; the system can, in fact, be quite flexible. In any case, an enthusiastic owner usually spends a good deal of time at week-ends or in the evenings on tuning and adjustments—or "profitable tinkering," as it has been aptly termed.

It is also advisable to have the car put on a garage hoist at least twice a year so that a thorough inspection of the underside can be made in reasonable comfort. Look especially for signs of rust developing in the underframe and floor, chafed or rusty brake lines, leaks from the exhaust system, loose nuts and bolts and for signs of accidental damage.

9

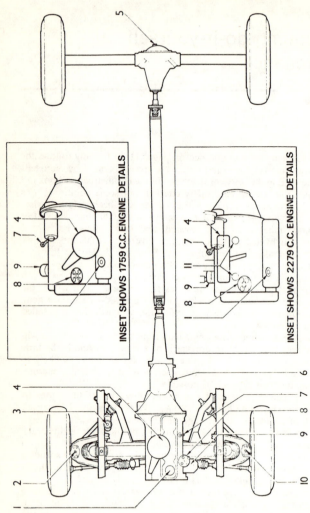

INSET SHOWS 1759 C.C. ENGINE DETAILS

INSET SHOWS 2279 C.C. ENGINE DETAILS

Fig. 1. Maintenance chart, showing most of the points which need attention on Viva and Magnum models

1, engine oil filler. 2, 10, front suspension arm ball joints. 3, brake fluid reservoir. 4, carburettor air filter. 5, rear-axle filler plug. 6, gearbox filler plug. 7, oil level dipstick. 8 ignition distributor. 9, engine oil filter. 11, carburettor hydraulic dampers

PLANNED HOME MAINTENANCE

Job Number		Page Number

Every 250 miles (400 km) or weekly

W-1	*Engine.* Check oil-level and top-up if necessary (check daily if engine is worn and also when refilling with fuel on a long run)	17
W-2	*Radiator.* Check water-level when cold and top-up if necessary . .	27
W-3	*Wheels and Tyres.* Check tyre pressures *when cold*. Watch for cuts and signs of uneven wear. Check tightness of wheel nuts	87–8
W-4	*Battery.* Check level of liquid in cells	90
W-5	*Windscreen Washer Reservoir.* Check level of fluid .	
W-6	*Brake Fluid Reservoir.* Check level of fluid (this is a precautionary check only—topping-up should be required only at long intervals, unless a leak has developed in system)	72

Every 3,000 miles (5,000 km) or every 3 months

Carry out Jobs W-1–W-6 and the following additional work

3-1	*Carburettor(s).* Stromberg carburettors: Top-up piston damper with oil. Check air valve piston for freedom. All carburettors: Check slow-running adjustments	46, 50
3-2	*Brakes.* Check pedal travel. Inspect brake pipes and hoses for leakage	73, 80
3-3	*Lighting System.* Check headlamp beam alignment, lamp glasses for cracks, side, tail and indicator lamps for blackened bulbs, rusty contacts and water in lampholders	93–5
3-4	**General Safety Check**	

With the car on ramps, on a garage hoist or over a pit, make a thorough inspection underneath. Check for:

1 Oil, brake-fluid and water leaks.
2 Rusting of the underside of the body, especially at the suspension mountings.
3 Rusty, leaking or damaged exhaust system.
4 Loose or worn propeller-shaft universal joints.
5 Damage to steering and suspension parts, split or displaced grease-retaining gaiters.
6 Loose nuts and bolts, especially those retaining the steering and suspension units, and the shock absorbers.
7 Cuts or bulges in the walls of the tyres.
   Also check the action and adjustment of the door, bonnet and boot latches and locks, and the condition of the seat belts and fastenings.

Every 6,000 miles (10,000 km) or every 6 months

Carry out jobs W-1–W-6 and 3-1–3-3 and following additional work

6-1	*Engine Lubrication.* Drain oil and refill sump	18
6-2	*Engine.* Renew oil-filter element.	19
6-3	*Engine.* Check valve-tappet clearances. Adjust if necessary . .	20
6-4	*Engine.* Check crankcase-breather filter. Service breather valve, when fitted	24
6-5	*Cooling System.* Check condition of hoses, and for leaks when engine is fast	28
6-6	*Fan and Dynamo Driving Belt.* Check belt tension. Adjust if necessary .	29
6-7	*Carburettor Air-cleaner.* Check condition of element . . .	47
6-8	*Sparking Plugs.* Clean; check and reset gaps	33
6-9	*Ignition Distributor.* Lubricate distributor. Clean or renew contact points—and adjust gap. Clean distributor rotor and cap . .	35, 36, 38

PLANNED HOME MAINTENANCE

Every 12,000 miles (20,000 km) or every 12 months

Carry out the 6,000-mile service and following additional work

Every 24,000 miles (40,000 km) or every 2 years

PLANNED HOME MAINTENANCE

4 The engine

ENGINE repairs and adjustments that can be tackled without the use of special tools and equipment are mainly influenced by the design of the cylinder head, valve-operating gear and, in the case of major overhauls, by the "bottom-half" components, the most important of which are the crankshaft, pistons and connecting-rods. A brief description of the main features of the engines will therefore be of interest to the practical owner who wishes to do as much of the work as possible.

The Viva and Magnum engines fall into two groups—those with push-rod-operated valve gear, in the 1,159 c.c. and 1,256 c.c. ranges, and the 1600, 1800 and 2300 models, which have overhead camshafts.

To distinguish between the two groups, the engines will be described, in this chapter, as *push-rod* or *overhead-camshaft* types.

The push-rod engines are well-tried designs, developed from the earlier HA and HB Viva power units, but modified to provide increased power by the use of larger inlet valves and the free-flow exhaust system of the earlier Viva 90 unit.

The overhead valves are operated by rockers and push-rods from a camshaft which is carried in the cylinder block. The rockers are unusual in being in the form of cupped steel pressings, each mounted on a hollow stud which is pressed into the cylinder head and retained by an adjustable nut which has a hemispherical seating. To adjust the valve clearance it is necessary only to turn the self-locking nut.

If a rocker retaining nut becomes slack, allowing the adjustment to alter in service, either the nut or the stud, or both, can be replaced without difficulty. The valve springs are retained by conventional cups and split-cone cotters.

The pistons have solid skirts and the offset piston pins or gudgeon pins are an interference fit in the upper ends of the connecting rods. When installing the pins, the eye of the connecting rod *only* must be heated evenly to 230–260°C, so that the eye will shrink on to the pin as it cools, and special tools are used to align the pin with the rod. Obviously a job for a Vauxhall dealer!

The crankshaft is carried in three main bearings, the upper half of the centre bearing being flanged to control the end-float of the shaft. The connecting rod and main bearings are of the modern thin-shell, steel-backed type, which can be replaced without the need for special fitting or scraping.

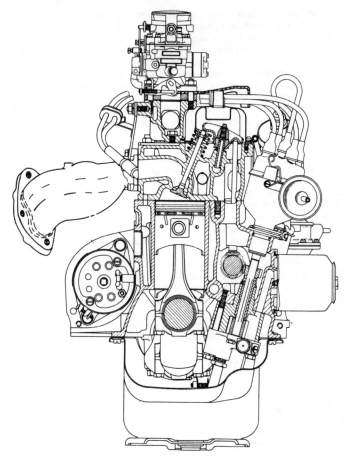

Fig. 2. This sectional view shows the components of the push-rod engine

The engines of the 1600 and 2300 models are of the single-over-head-camshaft design, first introduced in the Victor in 1,599 c.c. form and subsequently up-rated both in cubic capacity and power output. The only unorthodox feature of these engines is the use of a toothed, reinforced rubber belt to drive the camshaft and auxiliary shaft—something of a technical novelty when it was first introduced in the Victor, but which has since proved both efficient and extremely reliable in service.

The camshaft and tappets are carried in a housing which is bolted to the cylinder head, the cams operating the valves through inverted bucket tappets which incorporate wedge-shaped adjusting screws, thus overcoming the difficulty of valve-clearance adjustment in service, which is a problem with some other types of overhead-camshaft engines.

The cast-iron cylinder head is of the cross-flow type, with inlet ports on the right-hand side and exhaust ports on the left. The seatings of the sparking plugs are tapered to provide a gastight joint without the need for the usual sealing washers.

An auxiliary shaft, carried in two plain bearings in the cylinder block, and driven by the cogged belt, operates the fuel pump and drives the distributor and oil pump through skew gears.

The pistons have solid skirts and offset piston pins, which are an interference fit in the connecting rods, as in the case of the smaller engines—which means that removing and refitting the pins must normally be done by a Vauxhall dealer.

The crankshaft is carried in five main bearings and these, like the connecting-rod bearings, are of the thin-shell steel-back type. End-float on the crankshaft is controlled by a flange on the rear bearing.

Engine overhauls. Minor overhauls, such as decarbonizing and valve-grinding, are quite straightforward. Renewal of the bearings and the pistons also presents little difficulty (provided that a workshop manual is available), since the sump can be taken off without removing the engine. The engine can, however, be removed by lifting it out, complete with the gearbox or automatic transmission. If preferred, the engine can be parted from the gearbox or transmission and removed separately.

Further information concerning major overhauls and methods of saving money, either by using reconditioned units or employing specialist repairers, will be found in Chapter 13.

Fault-tracing. Even the best-maintained engine, of course, will sometimes display a fit of temperament, resulting in difficult starting, misfiring, loss of power and similar troubles. Simple fault-tracing is dealt with in Chapter 12, and most of the cures for the troubles that are likely to be encountered are dealt with in other chapters in this book.

ROUTINE ENGINE MAINTENANCE

The jobs described in this chapter are those listed in the maintenance schedule. Engine maintenance, of course, also includes a certain amount of work on the cooling system, ignition system and the carburettor and petrol pump. These jobs are dealt with in Chapter 5, 6 and 7.

Engine lubrication. The engine oil has been aptly described as the life-blood of the engine. It therefore pays to use a first-class lubricant. A "multigrade" oil is best. The correct grades are given on page 3.

Remember that the intervals between oil changes recommended in the maintenance schedule *applies only when a multigrade oil is used, under favourable conditions.* More frequent changes are advisable when most of the driving is done in cold weather, or when the car is used frequently for short runs and frequent starts are made from cold. At the other extreme, hot, dusty conditions will also cause rapid deterioration of the oil.

In such cases it is best to change the oil after 3,000 miles, or, in extreme cases, as frequently as every 1,000 miles.

Oil Pressure. When an oil-pressure gauge is not provided, the oil pressure warning lamp in the instrument panel will glow if the oil pressure should fall below a safe minimum figure. The lamp should, of course, light-up when the ignition is first switched on, but should be extinguished when the engine is running. If the lamp does not light-up, or does not go out when the engine is running, it is possible that the switch on the cylinder block which is operated by the oil pressure, is faulty. Either fit a replacement switch, or ask a garage to check the oil pressure by temporarily connecting a gauge to the switch union.

The correct oil pressure is given in Chapter 1. If the pressure is appreciably below this figure at normal speeds in top gear, with the engine thoroughly warmed-up, investigation is called for. Running the engine with too low a pressure can result in expensive damage to the crankshaft, main and connecting-rod bearings and other components.

Fortunately the oil pump is seldom at fault, except when the engine has covered a very large mileage, and the pick-up filter in the sump should not need cleaning between engine overhauls.

If satisfactory pressure is not restored when the above points have been attended to, the crankshaft and connecting-rod bearings are probably worn, calling for a partial or complete overhaul as described in Chapter 13.

Having dealt with some of the general aspects of engine lubrication, we can now consider in more detail the lubrication jobs that are specified in the home-servicing scheme.

W-1: Checking the Engine Oil Level

1 Switch off the engine and wait for several minutes before taking a reading with the dipstick.
2 Remove the dipstick and wipe it with a clean cloth.
3 Replace the dipstick to its full depth, withdraw it and note the level. If necessary, add oil to bring the level to the high mark.

Special Notes
The oil-level should be checked only when the car is standing on level ground. Always allow a few minutes for the oil to drain into the sump

after the engine has been switched off, or after oil has been poured into the filler; otherwise a misleadingly low reading will be obtained. It is more economical to keep the oil well topped-up than to allow the level to fall nearly to the low mark on the dipstick before adding more oil, but there is obviously not much sense in adding a pint or so just before the

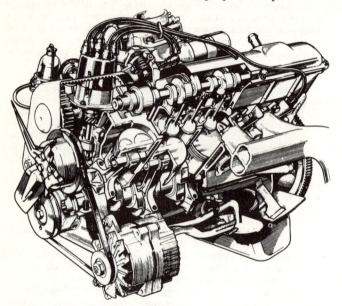

Fig. 3. The highly-efficient overhead-camshaft engine

oil is to be changed. Remember that the oil consumption may increase considerably during a fast run in hot weather. Check the level at each petrol stop.

6-1: Changing the Engine Oil

1 Make sure that the engine is thoroughly warmed-up.
2 Place a container which will hold about two gallons (to provide a safety margin) beneath the drain plug and unscrew the plug. Allow the oil to drain until the drips have ceased.
3 Clean the drain plug, check the copper washer is in good condition and replace the plug. Refill the sump and warm-up the engine.
4 Check for leakage at the drain plug. Re-check the oil-level with the car on level ground (Job No. W-1).

Special Notes

It is best to drain the oil when the car has just come in from a run. The oil will then be hot and fluid, and will be holding any impurities in suspension. If a good multigrade oil is used and changed at the recommended intervals it should not be necessary to clean out the engine with flushing oil. New multigrade oil will darken fairly quickly in service, but this merely indicates that the detergent in the oil is doing its job and is keeping the carbon and other particles in suspension.

An old kitchen washing-up bowl will serve as a drain pan, or a two-gallon tin with one side cut out. Allow sufficient time for the oil to drain completely before replacing the drain plug.

The oil filter element should be changed at every oil change.

6-2: Fitting a New Oil Filter

A full-flow, "throw-away" type of oil filter is fitted on all engines. On the push-rod unit, a renewable filter cartridge is enclosed in a metal casing which is retained by a single bolt. On overhead-camshaft engines, the canister which contains the filter element is screwed on to an adaptor on the crankcase and is replaced as a unit.

To fit a new filter to a push-rod engine:

1 Place a container beneath the filter to catch the oil which will run out when the filter casing is removed.
2 Unscrew the centre bolt and remove the casing, if necessary giving it a blow with the hand to break the joint at the crankcase seal.
3 Remove and discard the element. Do not attempt to remove the spring which fits over the centre bolt.
4 Wash the casing with paraffin, being particularly careful to remove any sludge deposits from the base of the casing, around and beneath the element seating plate and spring.
5 Remove the sealing washer from the crankcase housing and fit the new washer supplied with the replacement element. Install the element in the casing, refit the casing, being sure that it enters the groove in the crankcase, and tighten the bolt securely.
6 After refilling the engine sump, run the engine and check for oil leakage at the filter seal. Finally, recheck the oil level and top-up, if necessary, to compensate for the oil taken up by the filter.

To renew the filter on overhead-camshaft engines:

1 Place a container beneath the filter to catch the oil and unscrew the filter cartridge from the filter head. As the filter is often very tight, it may be necessary to use a strap wrench (which can be obtained from Halford branches and other accessory shops) to undo it. Alternatively, an obstinate filter can be unscrewed by tapping the blade of a screwdriver through it, thus providing extra leverage.

2 Make sure that the sealing washer is correctly positioned in the new filter and screw the filter home with hand pressure only. Excessive force should not be needed to ensure an oil-tight joint.

3 Refill the sump, run the engine and check for an oil leak at the filter joint. Recheck the oil level and if necessary top-up to compensate for the oil taken up by the filter.

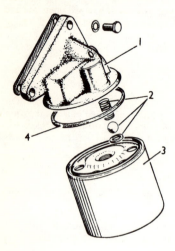

Fig. 4. The oil filter on overhead camshaft engines

1, filter adaptor. 2, filter pressure-relief valve. 3, replaceable filter cannister. 4, sealing ring

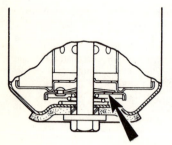

Fig. 5. Before installing a new element in the filter for a push-rod engine, check that the bypass holes (indicated by the arrow) are free from sludge

6-3: Valve Clearance Adjustment

To keep your engine in good tune, check the valve clearances at 6,000-mile intervals. If there is noticeable tapping or clicking from the valve cover on top of the engine, however, or if the car seems to lack power or liveliness the tappet clearances should be checked at once, without waiting for the routine service to fall due.

The term "tappet clearance" or "valve clearance" refers to the gap that must be maintained between the tip of the rocker or the tappet (which depresses the valve) and the valve stem itself. If the clearance is too small, the valve will be held open, because the parts expand as the engine warms up. This will cause loss of power and burnt valve seatings. If the clearances are too great, the valve gear will be noisy and the valves will open late and close early, seriously reducing power and maximum speed and increasing fuel consumption.

On push-rod engines the clearance must also be reset whenever the cylinder-head nuts are tightened down, as this compresses the cylinder head gasket and the resulting movement of the cylinder head reduces the valve clearances.

To check and adjust the clearances on push-rod engines:

The valve clearances must be adjusted while the engine is running. The pressed steel rockers operate on individual hollow studs pressed into the cylinder head. Each rocker is retained by a hemispherical ball seating and a self-locking nut. Screwing the nut down the stud will thus decrease the clearance between the tip of the rocker and the end of the valve stem, while unscrewing it will increase the clearance.

Fig. 6. Adjusting the valve clearance on a push-rod engine. The feeler gauge is inserted between the tip of the rocker and the valve stem

Before tackling the job for the first time, ask your local Vauxhall dealer to supply a suitable thin tubular spanner. At the same time buy strips of feeler gauge of the correct thicknesses for the engine, as given in Chapter 1. Checking the valve clearances while the engine is running can sometimes damage the blades of an ordinary set of feeler gauges; it is cheaper, therefore, simply to use a fresh section of the feeler strip.

The valve clearances should be checked *only when the engine is at its normal running temperature*. Four or five miles on the road should be sufficient to ensure that the temperatures of the cylinder block, cylinder head, valves, push-rods and rocker gear have become stabilized. It is not sufficient just to run the engine for a few minutes in the garage before checking the clearances.

1 Switch off, disconnect the breather hose from the valve cover, temporarily remove the sparking plug leads from the plugs and from the rocker cover retaining points, unscrew the valve cover retaining screw, and lift off the cover.
2 Refit the sparking plug leads to their respective plugs and start the engine. Unscrew the carburettor throttle-stop screw (*not* the idling mixture adjustment) to obtain as low an idling speed as possible.
3 Check the valve clearances with the correct feeler strip. Counting from the front of the engine, the inlet valves are Nos. 2, 3, 6 and 7. The exhaust valves are Nos. 1, 4, 5 and 8. It should just be possible to slide the feeler strip between the valve stem and the tip of the rocker as it rises; you should feel a slight drag. The strip will, of course, be nipped when the rocker compresses the valve spring.
4 If the gauge feels too slack or too tight, adjust the rocker nut until the correct clearance is obtained.

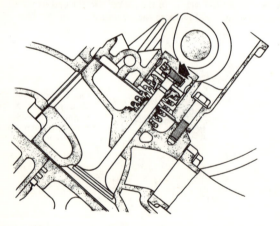

Fig. 7. On overhead-camshaft engines the valve clearances are adjusted by tapered screws, one of which is indicated by the arrow

To check and adjust the clearances on overhead-camshaft engines:

The valve clearances must be set with the engine fully warmed-up, but not running. The adjustment takes the form of a wedge-shaped screw in each tappet, which must be rotated with a $\frac{1}{8}$ in. Allen key, or with the special tool VR2041, available from your Vauxhall dealer, which makes the job rather easier.

1 Before checking and adjusting the clearances, the cam that operates the tappet being worked on must be set with its peak pointing away from the tappet, as shown in Fig. 8. Turn the engine crankshaft in a clockwise direction, using a spanner on the hexagonal-headed bolt which secures the crankshaft pulley.

2 Check the clearance between the base of the cam and the tappet. The exhaust valves are Nos. 1, 3, 5 and 7, counting from the front of the engine. The inlet valves are Nos. 2, 4, 6 and 8.

Fig. 8. Adjusting the valve clearance on an overhead-camshaft engine. The adjusting screw is rotated with an Allen key, shown inserted in the access hole in the tappet

3 If adjustment is necessary, rotate the tappet until the notch in its upper edge lines-up with the slot in the tappet housing, bringing the adjustment hole into line with the adjuster. Then turn the adjusting screw clockwise to decrease the clearance or anti-clockwise to increase it. The screw must be rotated through one or more complete turns, as indicated by a positive "click" at each revolution. Each full turn increases or decreases the clearance by 0·003 in. Intermediate settings are not possible.

Special Notes

In time, as the engine becomes worn, it may not be possible to obtain the correct clearance, owing to insufficient adjustment being provided by the tappet screw. Two sizes of undersize screw are available from Vauxhall dealers and the screws can be changed when the camshaft housing has been removed and the tappets taken out. The threads of a new screw should be smeared with graphited oil before it is fitted.

6·4: Cleaning Crankcase Ventilation Air Filter

The positive crankcase ventilation system used on these engines reduces air pollution, since the crankcase fumes are drawn back into the inlet manifold and burnt. Adequate ventilation also reduces the risk of corrosion and the formation of sludge inside the engine. On some earlier push-rod engines a ventilation air filter is mounted on the left side of the engine, serving also as a housing for the dipstick.

To clean the filter:

1 Withdraw the dipstick and unscrew the filter itself from the crankcase.
2 Wash the filter thoroughly in petrol or paraffin, shake it dry and oil the wire-gauze element inside the casing.
3 Allow the filter to drain for a few minutes before screwing it home and replacing the dipstick.

6-4: Servicing Crankcase Ventilation Valve

On some engines, a special crankcase ventilation valve is connected by a rubber hose to the rocker cover. This should be dismantled and cleaned at 6,000-mile intervals, but it is best to allow your Vauxhall dealer to do it, or at least to ask his advice before tackling the job. If the valve should stick or the spring should become weak (or be stretched by careless handling) the automatic ventilation of the crankcase will be upset and it may also be impossible to obtain satisfactory slow-running.

5 The cooling system

Maintenance of the cooling system could not be simpler, yet so often in a summer traffic jam, or on a mountain road, one sees cars stranded by the roadside with their bonnets raised while their drivers wait for their engines to cool down. What causes these "brew-ups"? A slack or broken fan belt, perhaps, or furred-up water passages, possibly a dud thermostat or an inefficient water pump. In this chapter we shall try to explain how the practical owner can avoid this sort of trouble by efficient maintenance.

How the System Works. A pressurized water cooling system is used on all models. The radiator filler cap incorporates a spring-loaded valve which opens when the pressure in the system reaches about 15 lb/sq in. (1·1 kg/sq cm), maintaining the coolant at well above atmospheric pressure and thus raising the boiling point to about 125°C (257°F) and reducing the risk of "brew ups" on steep hills and in traffic jams.

Because the system is under pressure when the engine is hot, the filler cap must be removed carefully (normally it is best to remove the cap only when the engine is cold). Otherwise, the sudden relief of pressure in the system may cause violent boiling and the eruption of a geyser or water and steam from the filler. *Pressure must always be released slowly*, as explained under "Topping-up the Radiator Header Tank."

A second spring-loaded valve in the expansion tank cap works in the opposite direction to the main valve, preventing the development of a vacuum in the cooling system when the engine cools down. If this valve were not provided, the hoses would collapse and the radiator might be damaged.

The water is circulated by a pump which is mounted at the front of the engine. Water is drawn from the base of the radiator, forced through the cylinder head and cylinder block and returned to the header tank at the top of the radiator. A current of air is blown through the radiator by a fan which is attached to the water-pump spindle and which is driven by a vee-belt from the crankshaft pulley.

When an automatic transmission is fitted, a cooler for the automatic transmission fluid is incorporated in the base of the radiator, but this is quite separate from the engine cooling system.

A thermostat (Fig. 9) is provided to restrict the flow of water to the radiator until the engine reaches its normal running temperature, thus, ensuring quicker warming-up and greater engine efficiency. More information about this thermostat will be found on page 29. When an interior heater is fitted, some of the water is bled off to pass through the radiator in the heater, before returning to the engine,

Although clean water can be used in the cooling system during the summer, anti-freeze solution must be used when there is any risk of frost. As a good anti-freeze preparation contains special inhibitors which prevent corrosion throughout the cooling system, however, there is everything to be said for using anti-freeze throughout the year. Further notes on this subject will be found on page 27, with a special caution regarding the use of Vauxhall anti-freeze and corrosion-prevention products.

Cooling-System Troubles. Apart from leakage, the troubles which are most likely to be encountered are overcooling or overheating of the engine. Overcooling is almost invariably caused by a faulty thermostat. It is a more serious fault than is generally realised and should be put right as quickly as possible, since it results in unnecessarily high fuel consumption and the risk of corrosion of the cylinder bores—apart from the discomfort of an inefficient heater during the winter months.

Overheating, probably the most common complaint as far as the cooling system is concerned, will occur if deposits of lime or rust are allowed to build-up in the water passages. Flushing the system, as described on page 30, will often cure the trouble, but remember that an unrestricted flow of air through the radiator is as important as a free flow of water. The small air passages often become clogged with an accumulation of dust and insects.

It may be possible for a garage to clean the passages by using a compressed-air gun *from the engine side of the radiator*, so that dust, gnats and flies are blown out by the air blast.

If flushing-out the system and blowing-out the air passages is unsuccessful, it will be necessary to remove the radiator, which is retained by four bolts, so that the film-block can be thoroughly cleaned—or renewed, if necessary—by a radiator specialist. The trouble may be caused by deposits of hard scale in the water passages, which will not respond to flushing or even to the use of a proprietory descaling compound, as described on page 31.

If the water pump is faulty, or water is leaking from the drain hole in the underside of the pump body, it is not too difficult to remove the pump and to fit a replacement. Don't try to overhaul the pump yourself. Dismantling it destroys the interference fit of the bearing, and even Vauxhall dealers are therefore told to fit a new pump.

Remember that overheating can be caused by faults other than those in the cooling system—*see* the chart on page 108.

Improving the Efficiency of the System. Although an engine-driven fan is needed to force air through the radiator when the engine is idling, or when driving slowly in traffic or climbing long hills, under most driving conditions the fan does little useful work, although it is absorbing engine power. The natural airflow through the radiator gives adequate cooling at normal road speeds.

It is for this reason that the fans on the Magnum models are driven by a viscous fluid in the fan hub. The drive "slips" at higher engine speeds, reducing the power absorbed and also the fan noise.

For other models, accessory firms have developed electrically driven fans, controlled by a thermostatic switch inserted in the top radiator hose or in the radiator header tank, which brings the fan into action only when necessary. An alternative is a fan, in which the pitch of the blades varies automatically with the engine speed.

ROUTINE MAINTENANCE

W-2: Topping-up the Cooling System
As already explained, the water-level should normally be checked when the system is cold. If the engine is hot, place a cloth over the filler cap and turn it *slowly* until the safety stop is reached. *Allow all steam or air pressure to escape*.

1 Press the cap downwards against the spring and rotate it further until it can be lifted off.
2 Top-up the radiator header tank until the water reaches the base of the filler.
3 Refit the filler cap and run the engine until it reaches normal temperature. Check for leaks.

Special Notes
When a cap is replaced it must always be tightened down fully—not just to the first stop.

If frequent topping-up is needed, check the system for leaks (*see* page 28). If anti-freeze is in use (*see* below) top-up with water/anti-freeze mixture and add the correct proportion of anti-freeze to the water in the expansion tank (if fitted). Most garages have special hydrometers to check the specific gravity of the solution in the cooling system—and thus the margin of safety—and will usually offer this service free of charge.

Using Anti-freeze. It is unwise to rely on draining-off the water when the car is not in use in cold weather, to prevent damage by frost. The interior heater, for example, is not drained by opening the drain plugs at the base of the radiator and in the cylinder-block. The safest plan is, therefore, to use an anti-freeze.

When a new car leaves the factory the cooling system is protected by Vauxhall corrosion preventive and Vauxhall anti-freeze. While there is nothing unusual in this—other manufacturers take similar precautions— it is important to remember that although Vauxhall corrosion preventive will mix with Vauxhall anti-freeze, it should not be used with any other anti-freezing preparation which has an ethylene-glycol base, as the mixture may form a soapy sediment which would clog the radiator and cause overheating. There is no reason, of course, why any other fully-inhibited anti-freeze should not be used in conjunction with another anti-corrosion preparation—such as "Bars Leaks," for example, which prevents corrosion and also seals leaks (*see* below).

While there will be no risk of a cracked cylinder block or a damaged radiator if an anti-freeze mixture is used in the proportions recommended in the accompanying table, the solution will form ice crystals at low temperatures which will prevent an adequate flow through the water pump and may cause severe overheating.

In these conditions the engine must be allowed to idle for at least five minutes after being started from cold, to allow the system to warm-up. To obtain complete protection at very low temperatures, equal volumes of anti-freeze and water are required. Except in arctic conditions, it will then be safe to drive the car away immediately after a cold start.

PROTECTION GIVEN BY ANTI-FREEZE MIXTURES

Anti-freeze (per cent in water)	Crystals begin to form		Solution is frozen solid	
	°C	°F	°C	°F
25	−13	9	−26	−15
33⅓	−19	−2	−36	−33
50	−36	−33	−48	−53

A first-class, fully-inhibited anti-freeze which complies with BS 3151 or 3152 can be left in the system for two years, but it is better to drain it off each spring and to refill with new anti-freeze, since the anti-corrosion inhibitors which are incorporated in the ethylene-glycol mixture slowly lose their effectiveness.

6-5: Checking the Cooling System for Leaks

It is often difficult to trace the source of a small leak which necessitates frequent topping-up of the radiator. Perished water hoses are likely culprits. Get the engine really hot and rev it up while carefully examining each hose. If the hoses seem to be sound, have the radiator pressure cap checked by a garage. It is a good plan to renew the hoses and the pressure cap every two years.

Sometimes internal seepage occurs past the cylinder-head gasket. Tighten the cylinder-head nuts progressively, *using a torque wrench, to the torque quoted on page* 4. If necessary, ask a garage to do this for you.

A preparation known as "Bars Leaks," obtainable from garages and accessory shops, will usually cure internal seepages and external leaks very effectively and it is an inexpensive precaution to add it to the cooling water whenever the system is flushed-out and refilled.

6-6: Adjusting the Fan and Alternator Driving Belt

The fan belt, which also drives the generator, should be kept correctly tensioned. It should be possible to deflect the centre of the belt between the generator and fan pulleys by about ½ in. (12·7 mm), using thumb pressure. If the belt is too slack, it will slip; if it is too tightly adjusted, excessive wear will occur on the fan and generator bearings. Check and if necessary adjust the tension only when the engine is cold.

To adjust the tension on the belt:

1 Slacken the nuts on the two mounting bolts on the alternator bracket and the bolt on the adjusting strut at the pulley end of the alternator.
2 Swing the alternator outwards to increase the tension in the belt, or inwards to decrease it.
3 Tighten the pivot bolts and strut bolts firmly.
4 Re-check the tension on the belt.

Special Notes

It is not advisable to use any leverage to move the alternator, unless the pivots and strut are binding, making it difficult to obtain sufficient tension on the belt by hand. *Lever only on the drive-end bracket.*

The belt must be kept free from grease or oil. If it develops a squeak or a whistle, dust it with French chalk, smear the edges with a little brake fluid or spray them lightly with silicone rubber lubricant from an Aerosol can.

Eventually the limit of the available adjustment will be reached and a new belt must be fitted. It is always advisable to carry a spare. A broken belt puts the fan, water pump and alternator out of action. In an emergency, a nylon stocking will serve as a get-you-home substitute for the belt.

The Thermostat. As explained earlier, the thermostat, which regulates the cooling-water temperature, vitally affects engine efficiency. Thermostats, of course, are not infallible and if overheating occurs, or if the engine is slow to warm-up, it is logical to check this item; but remember that overheating can be caused by a number of other faults (*see* the chart in Chapter 12).

12-8: Checking the Thermostat

The wax capsule type of thermostat is fitted under the domed cover which forms part of the water offtake pipe on the engine, and which is connected to the upper radiator hose.

To remove the thermostat:

1 Drain the cooling system to below the level of the thermostat.

2 Remove the securing bolts and swing the thermostat housing aside sufficiently to allow the thermostat to be extracted. The gasket should preferably be renewed.

3 If the thermostat valve is open, discard the unit and fit a replacement, which should be the wax-filled capsule type. If the valve is closed, place the thermostat in a pan of boiling water. If the valve does not open, the thermostat is faulty. If a kitchen thermometer is available, the opening temperature can be checked while moving the thermostat about in the pan of water. Do not let it rest on the bottom of the pan. When a new thermostat is tested, the valve should open at the temperature given in Chapter 1. A used thermostat will give slightly less-precise control of the cooling-water temperature.

4 When refitting the thermostat, clean the joint faces of the housing and use a new gasket if there is any doubt concerning the original. The word "Top" stamped on the flange of the thermostat must be uppermost.

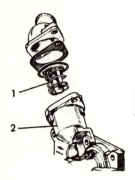

Fig. 9. The thermostat, 1, is housed in the water offtake casting on the water pump, 2

Special Notes

Before refitting a used thermostat, make sure that the small air-release hole in the valve is not choked and that it is at the highest point; otherwise an air-lock is likely to occur when the cooling system is refilled.

Many authorities recommend that the thermostat should be changed every two years as corrosion, deposits of sludge or hard scale, or a distorted valve, can all cause sluggish action.

12-8: Flushing and De-scaling the Cooling System

Once a year, or every 12,000 miles, the system should be drained, flushed-out and refilled.

Early models have drain taps in the cylinder block and the base of the radiator, but on later cars these are superseded by plugs. On still later models there may be no drain plug in the base of the radiator and it is then necessary to disconnect the lower radiator hose to drain the system.

1 Remove the radiator filler plug (*see* the caution on page 27). Open the drain taps or remove the drain plugs, and disconnect the bottom radiator hose, as the case may be. Set the interior heater control to "Hot."

2 Insert a hose in the filler neck and allow a gentle flow of water to pass through the system until clean water issues from the drains.

3 Close the drain taps or refit the plugs and reconnect the lower radiator hose if necessary. The threads of a drain plug should be smeared with a non-setting jointing compound before screwing the plug home. Refill the system slowly to prevent air-locks and if a heater is fitted, open the heater valve, slacken the heater water-return hose and run the engine until water flows from this hose. Tighten the hose clip while water is flowing, to prevent an air-lock in the heater.

4 Refit the radiator filler cap, run the engine for about half-a-minute, and top-up the system.

Special Notes

If water does not flow freely from the drains, probe them with wire to dislodge any sediment.

Before flushing the system it is an advantage to run the car for a day or two with a proprietary de-scaling compound added to the cooling water, to dissolve deposits of rust or scale. Apart from causing overheating, these deposits may be sealing minor leaks and if anti-freeze is used there is a risk that its very "searching" action may find such weak spots.

If straightforward flushing does not cure a persistent case of overheating ask a garage to remove the thermostat and reverse-flush the cylinder block and radiator separately, using a special flushing gun fed with water and air under pressure. If this is not successful, more drastic action will be required—*see* the notes on overheating given earlier.

If the cooling system is to be left empty for more than a short time, the cylinder block *must* be drained. If the system is only partly drained, the water-pump impeller seal face will become corroded and this will cause early failure of the water-pump seal and bearing when the car is put back on the road.

If the heater is inefficient after the system has been drained and refilled, there is probably an air-lock in the element. To clear this, detach the upper (return) hose from the heater to the engine at the engine end and plug the opening in the adaptor. With the radiator cap in place, hold the end of the hose higher than the heater and pour water into it until it overflows. Block the end of the hose with your thumb, remove the plug from the adaptor and refit the end of the hose.

6 The ignition system

Many otherwise competent do-it-yourself owners are apt to fight shy of the "electrics," so a simple description of the ignition system and the various components that will need attention from time to time will probably be welcomed by the non-technical average owner, especially as it will become evident that no specialized electrical knowledge is necessary for routine maintenance or simple fault-tracing. Those who are interested, however, will find more detailed explanations of the functions of the individual items in the system in other sections of this chapter.

Briefly, when the ignition is switched on, current flows from the battery through a low-voltage winding in the *ignition coil*. After leaving the coil, the current passes through a pair of *contacts* in the *contact-breaker*, inside the *distributor*, to the metal of the engine, before returning to the battery through the metal of the car and the negative battery lead.

When the starter motor turns the engine, the contact-breaker contacts —termed *"points"*— are opened and closed by a *cam* on a shaft in the distributor, which is driven by the engine. Whenever the points open, the flow of current in the low-voltage winding in the ignition coil is interrupted, causing a surge of high-voltage current in a *high-tension winding* in the coil. This surge (usually about 7,000–30,000 volts) is carried by a *high-tension cable* from the insulated cap of the coil to the central terminal in the moulded plastic *distributor cap*, from which it passes through a spring-loaded carbon contact to a *rotor* mounted on the top of the distributor spindle.

As the rotor turns, its tip passes close to terminals inside the distributor cap, which are connected to the *sparking-plug leads*. At the moment that the contact-breaker points open, the rotor will be pointing to a terminal in the cap and the correct plug will receive the surge of current. A spark then jumps across the *sparking-plug electrodes*, which project into the combustion chamber, firing the compressed mixture of petrol and air in the cylinder.

THE SPARKING PLUGS

The "tune" of an engine depends to a great extent on the sparking plugs. Only sound plugs, properly cleaned and correctly gapped, will give maximum performance and good fuel consumption. To keep old plugs in use until they are nearly worn-out is an expensive form of economy. They should be discarded after about 10,000–12,000 miles (16,000–20,000 km), although they may appear still to be serviceable. A new set costs less than half a tankful of petrol!

The sparking plugs fitted to push-rod engines are of the conventional 14-mm type. The overhead-camshaft engines, however, use a special type of plug which has a smaller hexagon than usual, calling for the use of a ⅝ in. AF plug spanner which can be obtained from a Vauxhall dealer. These plugs are not fitted with sealing washers. Instead, they have a tapered seat which forms a gas-tight seal, provided that the seating faces on the plugs and in the cylinder head are clean.

The workshop manual emphasizes that the tapered-seat plugs should be tightened to a torque of 15 lb/ft. Insufficient torque will prevent heat being dissipated from the plug and will cause pre-ignition, whereas over-tightening the plug may result in it seizing in the cylinder head. It is unlikely, however, that the average owner will possess a torque wrench and if the recommendation in the owner's handbook is followed—that the plugs should be tightened only by light hand pressure on the plug spanner tommy-bar—there should not be very much risk of either of these troubles occurring.

6-8: Cleaning and Adjusting the Sparking Plugs

The use of a garage plug-cleaner is the only really effective method of removing carbon and deposits from the internal surfaces and insulator. A fine abrasive, carried by a high-pressure air blast, thoroughly scours the interior of the plug, which can then be tested for sparking while under pressure—a much more stringent test than sparking across an air-gap.

To check the sparking-plug gaps and re-set them if necessary:

1 Pull off the connectors and unscrew the plugs. Keep the spanner square, to avoid cracking the external insulators.
2 Clean the points with a wire brush. If the internal insulators are dirty, or the plugs have been in service for more than 5,000 miles (8,000 km) have them cleaned by a garage.
3 Set the gap between the points to 0·030 in. (30 thousandths of an inch, 0·75 mm), using an inexpensive gauge and setting tool such as the Champion gap-servicing tool sold by accessory shops, and bending the *side* electrode only. If you must use pliers or a screwdriver, don't exert leverage against the central electrode. This may crack the internal insulator and the plug must then be scrapped.
4 Clean the threaded portion of each plug with a stiff brush and smear a trace of graphite grease on the threads.
5 Blow or wipe any dust or grit out of the plug recesses in the cylinder head. In the case of push-rod engines make sure that the sealing washers are in place and screw the plugs home by turning the plug spanner

without using the tommy-bar. Use the bar only for the final half-turn to ensure a gastight joint.

Special Notes

Over-tightening is unnecessary and is likely to lead to trouble. If the plugs cannot be screwed in easily by hand, ask your local garage to clean-up the threads in the cylinder head with a plug-thread tap, or make a tap by filing three or four v-shaped notches across the threads of an old plug, spaced around the plug so as to produce a series of cutting surfaces.

THE IGNITION COIL

Although a 12-volt electrical system is used on the Viva and Magnum range, the ignition coil operates on about 5–6 volts during normal running, when it is fed by a resistance wire incorporated in the wiring harness. When the starter motor is operating, however, the resistance wire is by-passed by a feed from the starter motor solenoid switch, more than compensating for the lower voltage which is caused by the very heavy current drain of the starter motor.

Remember to connect the white wire to the "+" terminal on the coil and the white and black wire to the "−" terminal.

The coil requires little or no attention, apart from keeping the external surface clean—particularly the moulded cap. A current which reaches a normal peak of about 12,000 volts (or more, if the plug gaps are too wide) will always try to find a leakage path from the central terminal to one of the low-tension terminals or to the earthed metal case of the coil. Moisture or greasy dirt is very liable to form such a conducting path.

A coil may be satisfactory when cold, or for a short period after the engine has been started, but may develop a partial or complete breakdown in the windings when it has become thoroughly warmed-up, causing mis-firing or ignition failure. As it will resume its normal action as soon as it cools down, this can often prove a very difficult fault to diagnose, but it will show up on an electronic test set. Otherwise, the only practicable test is to substitute, temporarily, a coil that is known to be in good condition.

THE IGNITION DISTRIBUTOR

As already explained, the distributor directs the high-tension current from the ignition coil to the sparking plugs in the correct firing sequence. It also contains a contact-breaker, which interrupts the low-voltage current passing from the battery through the ignition coil, and automatic-timing devices (described in more detail later) that vary the timing of the sparks at the plugs to suit the engine running-conditions at any moment.

The practical aspects of distributor servicing are quite straightforward, and the various parts can be easily identified in the illustrations.

Fig. 10. The sparking plug gap is best measured with one of the feeler gauges of a combination gap-setting and gauge tool, shown in Fig. 11

6-9: Lubricating the Ignition Distributor

Distributor fitted to a push-rod engine:

1 Remove the cap and pull the rotor off the end of the shaft.
2 Put two or three drops of oil on the felt pad in the hollow end of the rotor shaft.
3 Drip about a teaspoon of engine oil through the hole marked "Oil" in the contact-breaker baseplate.
4 Smear a trace of petroleum jelly on the cam.
5 Place a drop of oil on the contact-breaker pivot pin.
6 Refit the distributor cap.

Distributor fitted to an overhead-camshaft engine:

1 Remove the distributor cap.
2 Take out the screws and remove the rotor.
3 Put a few drops of engine oil through the hole marked "Oil" in the contact-breaker baseplate and a drop on each balance-weight pivot.
4 Smear a trace of petroleum jelly on the cam.
5 Refit the rotor, making sure that the square and the round peg enters the correct hole in the balance weight assembly.
6 Refit the distributor cap.

Special Notes

Too much or too little oil can cause trouble. If oil or grease finds its way on to the contact-breaker points, it will cause misfiring and difficult starting. On the other hand, if lubrication is neglected, excessive wear will occur on the moving parts, or the moving contact-breaker arm may bind on its pivot, again causing starting and misfiring troubles. If the automatic advance mechanism becomes dry or rusty, the engine performance and economy will suffer badly.

6-9: Inspecting the Distributor Contacts

On push-rod engines, the contact-breaker points can be examined after the rotor has been pulled off the end of the distributor shaft. On overhead-camshaft engines, the rotor is retained by two screws and the centrifugal advance mechanism is mounted above the contacts. With the rotor off, however, the contact breaker mechanism is quite accessible. Make a note that the correct location of the rotor on these engines is ensured by two pegs on its underside, one round and one square, which fit the respective holes in the balance weight driving plate.

To service the contacts:

1 Lever the pivoted contact arm away from the fixed contact. The contact surfaces should have a clean, frosted appearance, apart from a small "pip" and crater.
2 If the contacts are dirty or seem to be badly pitted, lever the slotted end of the spring on the moving arm clear of the retaining pips on the insulator and pull the moving arm off its pivot. Lift the two wires off the insulator, remove the single retaining screw, or the pair of screws, which retain the fixed contact plate and remove the plate.
3 If the contacts are merely oily, they can be cleaned with petrol, but if they are burnt or badly pitted, it is better to fit a new set. Contacts which have been refaced with a carborundum stone or a file seldom last very long.
4 Reassemble the contacts, making sure that the fixed contact plate is pressed firmly down on to the collar at the base of the moving arm pivot pin, and that the terminals on the two wires are replaced in the correct sequence, as shown in Fig. 12.

6-9: Adjusting the Contact-breaker Gap

When the new contact-breaker points have been fitted or the old points have been cleaned-up and refitted, the gap should be adjusted.

1 Turn the engine until the fibre block is exactly on the crest of one of the "humps" of the cam. A slight movement of the cam in either direction will give a false reading.
2 Slacken the screw or screws retaining the fixed-contact plate and move the plate by inserting a screwdriver blade in the notch in its edge. Set the gap to 0·020 in. (20 thousandths of an inch, 0·50 mm) with a feeler gauge, turning the screwdriver blade anti-clockwise to reduce the gap or clockwise to increase it.
3 Tighten the securing screw. Re-check the gap.

Special Notes

The gap between the contact-breaker points should never be measured with a feeler gauge unless the points have previously been trued-up. After only a few hundred miles of running, a small "pip" forms on one point and a corresponding "crater" on the other, owing to the transference of microscopic particles of metal by the spark that occurs whenever the points open. The "pip" renders it impossible to obtain a correct reading with a feeler gauge.

Badly-burnt or pitted points should always be renewed. It is difficult to keep the surfaces square when truing them up with a carborundum stone.

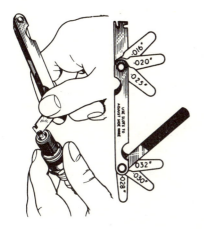

Fig. 11. Using a Champion gap-setting tool (right) to adjust the sparking-plug gap

A Remax contact-setting gauge (obtainable from most accessory shops) makes contact-breaker adjustment much easier, since there is no need to turn the engine in order to position the cam accurately before-checking the gap.

The Ignition Condenser or Capacitor. If the contact-breaker points are badly burned, the trouble may be due to too small a gap (which will seriously reduce the life of the points), but in most cases it is logical to suspect the condenser, or the capacitor, as it is more correctly termed.

This is connected across the contact points to absorb the surge of current, from 100–300 volts, that builds up in the primary winding of the ignition coil (in addition to the current induced in the high-tension winding which provides the spark at the sparking plug) and which would otherwise cause a destructive arc across the contact-breaker points, instead of the normal slight spark. The capacitor also discharges back through the primary windings, causing a more rapid collapse of the magnetic flux and a more intense spark at the sparking plug.

An inefficient capacitor, therefore, will not only cause rapid burning of the points, but will also result in a weak spark or—if it should short-circuit internally—failure of the plugs to fire at all.

The best test is to substitute a new capacitor for the doubtful. But make sure also that there is no break or short-circuit in the flexible lead that connects it to the contact-breaker terminal post. This cause of misfiring or complete cutting-out of the ignition is often overlooked. It is a sound insurance against possible trouble to fit a new capacitor whenever the contact-breaker points are renewed. It is not an expensive item.

6-9 (contd.): Cleaning the Distributor Rotor and Cap

The high-tension current from the coil enters the centre of the distributor cap and passes to the rotor through a spring-loaded contact. From the brass tip of the rotor the current jumps to each of the terminals in the distributor cap to which the sparking-plug leads are connected, in the sequence that gives the correct firing order—*see* Chapter 1.

1 Lightly scrape the contact strip on the rotor and the terminals inside the cap to expose bright metal. *Do not file them or rub them down with emery paper.*
2 Check the spring-loaded carbon contact inside the distributor cap. This sometimes sticks. Do not overstretch the spring.
3 Wipe the interior of the cap with a cloth moistened with methylated spirits (denatured alcohol) to remove dust or oily deposits, which will provide a leakage path for the high-tension current. A cracked cap or condensed moisture on the inside or outside of the cap is a common cause of difficult starting and misfiring.
4 Examine the rotor for signs of "tracking" (*see Special Notes*). If the tip of the terminal is badly burnt, fit a new rotor.

Special Notes

If current has been leaking between the terminals it will have left evidence in the form of dark tracks on the surface of the plastic. Sometimes these can be removed by a thorough cleaning with metal polish, but bad "tracking" usually calls for renewal of the cap or rotor.

6-9 (contd.): Testing the Distributor Cap and Rotor

There is a simple way to check the cap for tracking, without using special test equipment:

1 Detach two alternate sparking-plug leads, and the distributor-end of the coil high-tension lead, from the cap. Insert the end of the coil lead into each of the empty sockets in turn. Leave the remaining leads in place and connected to sparking plugs.

2 Switch on the ignition, make sure that the contact-breaker points are
  closed, and with the tip of a screwdriver flick the points apart. If there
  has been any tracking, a spark will jump across the interior of the
  distributor cap.

The rotor can be checked for breakdown of the insulation as follows,
without removing it from the cam spindle:

1 Remove the coil high-tension lead from the distributor cap.

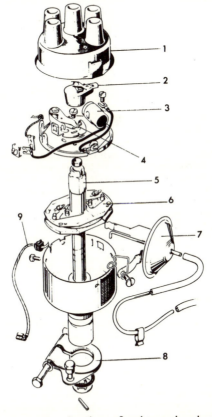

Fig. 12. The ignition distributor fitted to push-rod engines

1, distributor cap. 2, rotor. 3, condenser or capacitor. 4, contact-breaker assembly. 5, cam. 6, centrifugal timing control. 7, vacuum timing control. 8, distributor clamp. 9, low-tension connection

2 Hold it almost in contact with the edge of the rotor blade and flick the contact-breaker points open. If the rotor is faulty a spark will jump the air gap between the high-tension lead and the rotor blade.

Special Notes

Occasionally, internal leakage develops from the underside of the brass electrode of the rotor, through the plastic to the interior surface, allowing the high-tension current to jump to the cam spindle and so to earth. This can be a very elusive fault to spot but will be revealed by the above test. Fit a new rotor whenever you fit new sparking plugs and you should have no trouble.

The High-tension Leads. On the high-tension side of the ignition system, we are dealing with very high voltage (7,000–30,000 volts or more) which will "flash over" or take the line of least resistance whenever possible. The high-tension leads between the coil and the distributor and between the distributor cap and the sparking plugs must, therefore, be renewed when a test, made by doubling the cable between the fingers and examining the surfaces for tiny cracks, indicates that they have deteriorated. Don't wait until misfiring sets in.

Don't be tempted to use ordinary rubber-covered high-tension cable. Make sure that you get the modern type containing carbon-impregnated nylon or cotton cords which form high-resistance conductors, to suppress ignition interference with radio and television sets. These cables (which are obtainable from your dealer) must *not* be cut and no attempt should be made to fit new terminals to them—the result will be a poor contact which will spark inside the insulation and burn the conductor away. *Complete sets of cables must be fitted as supplied.* Misfiring or difficult starting can often be traced to a faulty ignition cable.

IGNITION TIMING

The timing of the spark varies under running conditions. It must occur earlier as the engine speed increases but must be retarded, to prevent detonation or "pinking," when the engine is under load. Two automatic controls are therefore provided. Both are of vital importance to ensure maximum performance and satisfactory fuel consumption.

The first, a centrifugal control which responds to engine speed, is in the form of two small weights below the contact-breaker baseplate in the distributor. Provided that it receives regular lubrication, the centrifugal timing control seldom gives trouble. If a spring should break, it is essential to renew both springs. *Make sure that they are of the correct part number for the engine.* Their strength determines the shape of the advance curve, giving the correct amount of advance for any speed.

Vacuum Timing Control. The circular housing beside the distributor body contains a flexible diaphragm. It is connected by a pipe to a point in the carburettor, near the edge of the throttle, so that the diaphragm is influenced by the fluctuating partial vacuum in the induction system when the engine is running at all speeds above the idling setting.

At moderately high engine speeds, with the throttle partly closed—under main-road cruising conditions, for example—a relatively high vacuum exists and the control advances the timing. When the engine is pulling hard at low speeds with a wide throttle opening, the vacuum is low and the diaphragm is returned by spring pressure. The contact-breaker assembly then rotates anti-clockwise and the spark occurs later.

It will be seen that the action of the vacuum control either adds to, or opposes, the action of the centrifugal control, ensuring the most effective timing under all conditions of load and speed.

6-9: Checking the Vacuum Timing Control

Check the following points:

1 Make sure that the suction chamber does not contain any condensed fuel. Test the action of the diaphragm by applying suction to the union. If the diaphragm appears to be faulty, fit a new unit.

2 Check the rubber connections at each end of the vacuum pipe and renew them if they have split or are a loose fit on the pipe. This is very important. Even a slight air-leak will affect the action of the control.

3 Renew the pipe if it has been kinked by careless work on the engine.

6-10: Setting the Ignition Timing

The basic ignition timing can never be completely "lost" if a special point is made of checking, *before* removing the distributor, the position of the distributor body in relation to the engine, and also the direction in which the rotor is pointing when the engine is set with No. 1 piston at top-dead-centre on the compression stroke and the timing marks are correctly aligned as described below—

On the 1,159 and 1,256 c.c. engines there is a pointer on the rear flange of the crankshaft fan pulley, which lines-up with two projections on the timing case. Viewed from the front of the engine, the right-hand projection indicates top-dead-centre, and the left-hand projection, 9 deg. before top-dead-centre. To obtain the correct timing of 4½ deg. b.t.d.c. for an engine with standard compression ratio, therefore, the pointer on the pulley must be midway between the two projections. To time the ignition to 9 deg. b.t.d.c. (for a low-compression engine only), line-up the pointer with the left-hand projection.

On overhead-camshaft engines, either a notch in the rear flange of the fan pulley or (when a pressed steel pulley is used) a pointer projecting from the edge of the pulley, registers with two timing marks which are impressed in the timing belt cover. The lower mark indicates 9 deg. before top dead centre and the upper mark, t.d.c.

So much for the timing indicator. To carry out the job if the distributor has been removed from the engine, follow operations 1–4 below. If the distributor has not been removed, only operations 1, 3 and 4 are necessary.

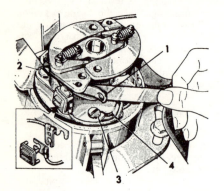

Fig. 13. Checking the contact-breaker gap on an overhead-camshaft engine

1, contact points. 2, 3, contact plate screws. 4, notch for screwdriver blade when adjusting gap

1 Remove the sparking plugs and the valve cover and turn the crankshaft clockwise (as viewed from the front of the engine), until both valves of No. 1 cylinder (nearest to the radiator) are closed—i.e., No. 1 piston is on the compression stroke. Align the timing mark with the pointer as described above. If you overshoot the correct position, turn the engine through another full revolution clockwise—don't turn it backwards, as the slack in the timing chain will give a misleading setting.

2 *Push-rod engines*: Check that the slot in the oil pump spindle, which drives the distributor, is offset to the rear of the engine; that is, the thicker segment of the shaft should be forwards. Rotate the distributor rotor so that the driving tongue on the shaft will engage with the slot in the pump spindle. Slide the distributor into place, with the bolt in the clamp plate. The vacuum control housing should be pointing away from the ignition coil and should be just above the oil filter. Fit the set-screw that secures the clamp plate to the crankcase.

Overhead-camshaft engines: When the distributor is correctly installed the rotor should be pointing upwards, in the "12 o'clock" position, and the vacuum timing control should be towards the fuel pump. Since the driving gears will rotate the rotor shaft slightly as the distributor is slid into place, begin with the rotor at the "11 o'clock" position.

3 Make sure that the centrifugal advance weights are not binding, by turning the rotor anti-clockwise and releasing it. Check that the contact-breaker baseplate is free to rotate slightly.

4 Set the timing by rotating the distributor body anti-clockwise until the contact points are just closed and then slowly turn it clockwise until they just separate. If the ignition is switched on, a small spark can be seen and heard to jump across the points as they separate.

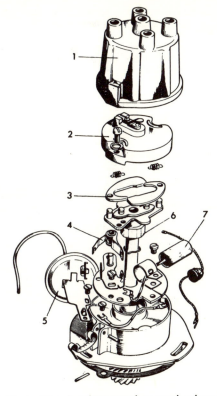

Fig. 14. The ignition distributor used on overhead-camshaft engines

1, distributor cap. 2, rotor. 3, centrifugal timing control. 4, contact-breaker. 5, vacuum timing control. 6, cam. 7, condenser or capacitor

If it is necessary to turn the distributor through a considerable angle from the initial position in which it was fitted, the gears are not meshing correctly, being one or more teeth out. Withdraw the distributor and refit it correctly as described above. When the right timing has been obtained, tighten the clamping bolt to prevent the distributor body from rotating and then re-check the timing. *Do not overtighten the bolt.*

Special Notes

A more accurate method of timing is to connect a side-lamp bulb, mounted in a suitable holder, across the two low-tension terminals on the top of the ignition coil. When the points are closed the lamp will light up. At the instant that they open, it will be extinguished. When checking the opening point, keep a light finger pressure on the rotor in a clockwise direction to take up backlash in the drive. Tighten the clamping bolt and re-check the timing.

It must again be emphasized that the timing must not be set immediately after turning the engine backwards. The backlash in the timing chain and distributor driving-gears will cause an appreciable error. Always turn the engine clockwise when making the final adjustment.

6-10 (contd.): Adjusting the Timing on the Road

As mentioned earlier, the static setting should be regarded only as the starting point for a series of road tests during which the timing can be adjusted, advancing or retarding the ignition slightly to suit the condition of the engine and the octane number (anti-knock rating) of the fuel that will normally be used.

The ignition timing is extremely critical and it is only too easy to overdo this adjustment. The usual fault is to set the ignition too far advanced. While the engine may feel very lively, it will probably be rough and the pistons and bearings will suffer. In actual fact, the overall performance and fuel consumption will not be as good as when the ignition is correctly timed.

The best ignition setting is that which gives the shortest time to accelerate over the speed range of, say 30–60 m.p.h. in top gear. It will also give the most economical fuel consumption.

7 The carburettor and petrol pump

ROUTINE maintenance of the carburettor and petrol pump is quite straight-forward and carburettor adjustment should not be too difficult for a practical owner, although it is a fact that an unnecessarily large proportion of cars fitted with Stromberg carburettors are giving less than their maximum performance and fuel economy, owing to poor carburettor adjustment. This subject is therefore dealt with fully in this chapter.

Another important point concerns the efficiency of the carburettor itself. After a large mileage, such parts as the throttle spindle and bearings, air valve diaphragm, jet and jet needle inevitably become worn, and engine performance is bound to suffer. A worn carburettor can be exchanged for a new one at a reasonable cost, however, and this may prove to be a good investment after a car has covered, say 40,000 miles or more.

Similarly, if the petrol pump gives trouble, it is usually more satisfactory to fit a reconditioned replacement under the service-exchange scheme. Although it is possible to buy pump repair kits, strictly speaking the pump should be tested for rate of flow, suction and pressure after overhaul, and this calls for the use of special equipment. If the pump is delivering too little petrol, for example, a few miles at full throttle on a motorway might result in a hole being burnt through a piston crown, owing to the very high flame temperature caused by the weak carburettor mixture.

Types of Carburettor. Two radically different types of carburettor are fitted to the engines in the Viva and Magnum range. The Zenith 30IZ and 36IV carburettors (with their variants on the basic type), are termed "static" carburettors, since fuel metering is carried out by means of fixed jets.

The Zenith-Stromberg CD carburettors, on the other hand, are of the "constant depression" type (hence CD). In these, a single jet is used, and the opening at the top of the jet is varied by a tapered needle which is clamped in the base of a piston or air valve which rises and falls as the airflow through the carburettor (which causes a depression or semi-vacuum in the carburettor throat) varies with changes in engine speed and throttle opening.

The Zenith and Zenith-Stromberg carburettors will be described in more detail later in this chapter, when dealing with carburettor servicing, but it might be as well to clear up some points regarding the codes which indicate the different variants listed in the specifications on page 3, as these often confuse owners.

The number indicates the size or capacity of the carburettor and, in the case of static carburettors, IZ or IV, the basic type. When additional letters are used they mean: T, water-heated automatic choke instead of manual type. E, emission-controlled carburettor meeting specifications for restriction of exhaust pollution.

With Stromberg carburettors, CD is the basic type. The additional letters are: S, disc-type manually-operated starting carburettor. T, thermostatic control of starting carburettor. E, emission-controlled carburettor. V, spring-loaded metering needle instead of fixed needle.

ROUTINE MAINTENANCE

Before dealing with carburettor servicing and adjustment, we can dispose of the simple routine maintenance jobs for the fuel system.

3-1: Topping-up the Carburettor Piston Damper—Zenith-Stromberg Carburettors

There is a small hydraulic damper, consisting of a piston, fitted with a one-way valve and working in an oil-filled recess, in the depression-chamber cover that forms the upper part of the carburettor. The damper

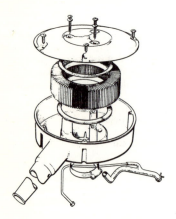

Fig. 15. A typical air cleaner, containing a pleated-paper element. Other types are very similar

prevents the carburettor piston from rising too quickly when the throttle is opened suddenly, which would cause an unduly weak mixture and a "flat spot" during acceleration. The damper also prevents the piston "fluttering" under certain running conditions.

To top-up the damper:

1 Remove the air cleaner.
2 Unscrew the plastic cap and withdraw the damper.
3 Insert a finger in the air intake and lift the air valve so that the level of the oil in the hollow guide rod can be checked. It should be within ¼ in. (6 mm) below the top of the hollow guide rod. If necessary, top-up with engine oil.
4 When refitting the damper, the small collar surrounding the damper rod must be fitted into the guide rod. To do this, insert the damper in the guide rod, allow the air valve to drop, screw down the plastic cap and again lift the air valve in order to press the collar into the hollow guide rod. Check that it is properly seated by lifting the air valve and unscrewing and raising the plastic cap just sufficiently to allow the top of the guide rod to be seen.

Special Notes

Do not use thin machine oil, upper-cylinder lubricant or a heavy oil in the damper. The point is stressed because some garage mechanics do not seem to be aware of the important of using the correct grade of engine oil. If the performance is sluggish or "spitting back" occurs when the throttle is suddenly opened and the engine is at its normal operating temperature, check that the oil-level in the damper is not low and that the right grade of oil has been used. Don't necessarily wait until the 6,000-mile service to make this check. Sometimes the oil disappears more quickly—hence the preventive check at 3,000 miles.

12-2: Renewing the Carburettor Air-filter Element

Although the air-filter element should be changed during the 12,000-mile service, it may be necessary to renew it after a lower mileage has been covered if the car is operating in very dusty conditions or if the element has acquired a greasy coating, caused by condensed crankcase fumes. A clogged air-filter will reduce engine performance and increase the petrol consumption.

To change the element in a single-carburettor cleaner:

1 Remove the air cleaner from the carburettor. If the cleaner has a plastic container, remove the top cover, which is a snap fit on the body, by twisting the edge of a coin in the groove between the cover and the body. With metal filter bodies, undo the screws that retain the top cover.
2 Remove and discard the old element. Clean the interior and exterior of the body and cover thoroughly.
3 Check the condition of the sealing washers.
4 Fit the replacement element and replace the cover, noting that the

longer screws which retain a metal cover fit the three holes in the centre of the cover.

5 In the case of a plastic cleaner, which has an adjustable air intake tube, turn the tube so that it points down towards the exhaust manifold in winter, and towards the outside of the engine compartment in summer.

Fig. 16. The air cleaner intake tube on 1,159 c.c. and 1,256 c.c. engines should point downwards in winter and be turned to the dotted position in summer

Special Notes

The "Winter" setting should normally be used only in cold weather, but the fact that the air is drawn from close to the exhaust manifold will also help to prevent the carburettor icing-up internally during mild weather conditions, especially when the humidity of the air is high. The "Summer" position provides a supply of cooler air which enables the engine to develop maximum power.

To renew the element on twin-carburettor engines:

1 Remove the bolt and two nuts which secure the cleaner to the adaptor plates on the carburettors.
2 Separate the two halves of the cleaner body and discard the elements.
3 Clean the inside and outside of the body.
4 Check that the sealing washers are correctly fitted to the adaptor plates and that the plain washer, sleeve and seal are assembled, in that order, on the attachment bolts.
5 Fit the two new elements and reassemble the cleaner, placing a sealing washer, followed by a plain washer, beneath the bolt on each of the studs.

12-3: Cleaning the Petrol-pump Filter

The petrol pump is mounted accessibly on the left-hand side of the engine on the smaller power units, and on the right-hand side on the overhead-camshaft engines. In the course of a year's running a certain amount of sediment and perhaps a few globules of water will accumulate in the base of the filter chamber and the filter gauze itself may be partly clogged.

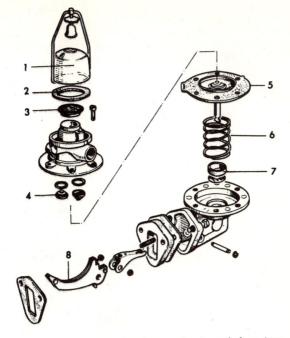

Fig. 17. The fuel pump fitted to overhead-camshaft engines

1, filter bowl. 2, gasket. 3, filter gauze. 4, inlet and outlet valves. 5, diaphragm. 6, operating spring. 7, seal. 8, operating lever

To clean the filter:

1 Thoroughly clean the petrol-pump externally.
2 On the smaller engines, remove the setscrew that retains the domed metal filter cover. On overhead-camshaft units, slacken the thumb-nut that retains the glass filter bowl, swing the wire clamp aside and lift off the bowl. In each case check the condition of the cork sealing washer.
3 Lift the gauze filter out of its recess. Mop out any water or sediment which has accumulated in the base of the filter chamber. Swill the gauze filter in petrol but do not use a fluffy rag or a wire brush to clean it.
4 Check the soundness of the petrol-pipe connections and look for any signs of petrol leakage.

5 Refit the filter gauze, sealing-washer and cover, and tighten the retaining nut sufficiently to prevent air or petrol leakage past the gasket, but do not overtighten it.

6 Run the engine for a few minutes and re-check the filter for any signs of leakage. This test will show up a faulty sealing ring.

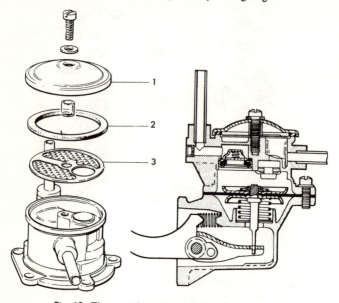

Fig. 18. The petrol pump used on push-rod engines
1, filter cover. 2, gasket. 3, filter gauze

Special Note

An air leak at the filter-cover flange is one of the most common causes of petrol starvation, due to insufficient output from the pump. Renew the gasket if there is the slightest doubt about its condition.

3-1: Slow-running Adjustments

The increasingly stringent regulations concerning exhaust-gas pollution which have been introduced during the last few years have resulted in the development of precisely calibrated emission-controlled versions of the basic Zenith and Zenith-Stromberg carburettors in which the idling mixture adjusting screw is sealed. If adjustment becomes necessary in service, this should be done only by using specialized exhaust-gas analysis equipment, in order to keep within the specified limits for emissions. Obviously, this must be a job for your Vauxhall dealer.

Fortunately, however, the regulations regarding emission-controlled engines demand that these carburettors shall retain their tune over an operating life of at least 50,000 miles, so it is unlikely that adjustment will be required—unless, of course, a carburettor has been completely stripped or has been tampered with by someone who does not understand the principles involved.

This does not apply, however, to the majority of Viva and Magnum engines in use at present in the UK. Provided that the mixture adjustment screw has not been locked by a wire and a lead seal, or has not been blanked-off by a thimble-shaped cover, slow-running adjustments may be carried out as follows:

To adjust the idling speed and mixture strength on Zenith "static" carburettors:

The strength of the slow-running mixture considerably influences acceleration from low speeds. If there is a "flat-spot" just as the throttle is opened from the idling position, try the effect of slightly enriching the slow-running mixture as described on page 52. A fraction of a turn of the screw may be sufficient. It will probably be necessary to adjust the stop screw slightly to prevent "lumpy" idling, but an idling setting that is slightly on the rich side is an advantage.

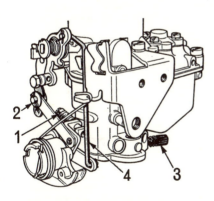

Fig. 19. Typical adjustments on a Zenith "static" carburettor

1, throttle stop screw. 2, acceleration pump link. 3, idling mixture control screw. 4, throttle-choke interconnecting rod

Remember that it will be impossible to obtain good idling if ignition or mechanical faults exist.

The throttle stop-screw controls the amount by which the throttle approaches the closed position and therefore regulates the slow-running speed. The richness of the slow-running mixture is determined by the mixture-control screw, a richer mixture being provided when the screw is turned anti-clockwise. Both these adjustments are shown at 1 and 3 in Fig. 19.

1 With the engine at normal running temperature, turn the mixture-control screw in an anti-clockwise direction to enrich the mixture, until the idling becomes unsteady and the engine runs with a rhythmic beat.

2 Turn the screw clockwise until the engine passes through the smooth idling range and begins to misfire slightly. The exhaust will now have a "splashy" note and the gas will be odourless.

3 Midway between these points will be the ideal slow-running mixture.

4 Readjust the throttle-stop screw to restore the correct idling speed.

5 If necessary, slightly readjust the mixture-control screw.

Special Notes

It is better to set the carburettor with the mixture *very slighty* rich—that is, with the engine just "hunting" slightly—as this setting will give the best pick-up on snap throttle openings from low speeds, without appreciably increasing the fuel consumption.

If the mixture is set on the weak side, not only will there be a hesitation when the throttle is opened just above the idling point but explosions may occur in the exhaust system when the throttle is closed at fairly high speeds. This trouble, incidentally, will be aggravated by air leakage at any point in the system. It should be rectified as soon as possible, because there is a risk of the silencer being split if a particularly violent explosion should occur.

Finally, remember that with modern small engines, one should not expect to obtain a very slow and even idling setting. It is better to keep the idling speed slightly on the high side, particularly if the engine is worn, as there will be less likelihood of the plugs becoming oiled-up during long periods of idling in traffic and the engine will accelerate better from very low speeds.

To adjust the fast-idling speed on Zenith "static" carburettors:

On IZ carburettors there is an adjustment at the upper end of the rod that connects the choke to the throttle, opening the latter slightly and providing a high idling speed when the choke is in use. This should not be disturbed unnecessarily. If the original setting is lost, the correct method of carrying out the adjustment is to remove the carburettor from the engine, insert a No. 61 drill between the throttle flap and the body, with the throttle stop-screw unscrewed so that the flap can close against the drill. The choke lever should be held against its stop, allowing the choke flap to be fully closed.

In practice, however, it is usually possible to achieve a satisfactory setting of the lever by trial-and-error methods, the object being to obtain an idling speed which is sufficiently high to prevent the engine stalling when the choke is in use, but which will not cause the engine to race when the choke control is pulled out fully, or hold the throttle slightly open when the choke control is pushed home.

On other Zenith carburettors, the fast-idle setting is determined by the length of the interconnecting rod. Provided that this has not been bent, the correct setting is automatically obtained.

To adjust the idling speed and mixture strength on Zenith-Stromberg carburettors:

The correct adjustment of the slow-running mixture strength is particularly important on Stromberg carburettors. As explained earlier, the richness of the idling mixture is determined by slightly raising or lowering the jet in relation to the tapered needle, which is at its lowest point when the engine is idling. But any alteration in the height of the jet must also effect, to some extent, the mixture strength over the whole range of engine speed and throttle opening.

Too rich a mixture will be reflected in heavy fuel consumption, while too weak a setting will reduce the power available and may cause burnt valves and, possibly, damage to the pistons.

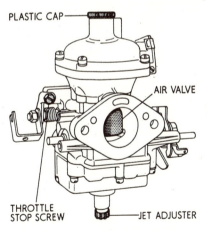

PLASTIC CAP

AIR VALVE

THROTTLE
STOP SCREW

JET ADJUSTER

Fig. 20. Adjustment and servicing points on a Zenith-Stromberg carburettor

Non-technical owners may prefer to stop reading at this point, since the rest of the jobs described in this chapter call for a good deal of know-how. If in doubt, leave the work to an experienced mechanic (and this does *not* include the well-meaning youngsters in some garages who insist on twiddling the adjusting screws with more enthusiasm than skill!).

The throttle-stop screw controls the idling speed and the jet adjusting-screw regulates the mixture strength. When turned clockwise it weakens the mixture. The method is the same when a single carburettor or twin carburettors are fitted, but twin carburettors must also be synchronized as described on page 55.

1 It is to begin the adjustment from a basic setting. Bring the engine up to its normal working temperature, remove the air cleaner, unscrew and remove the hydraulic dashpot plunger and insert a pencil in the bore so that the air valve can be held down on to its seating on the bridge in the throttle passage.

2 Screw the jet adjustment screw upwards—the edge of a coin is ideal for this purpose—until the jet just contacts the underside of the air valve, as indicated by increased resistance to screwing-up the jet. If the jet screw is stiff to turn, it is difficult to judge when it makes contact with the air valve. In this case, shine a torch beam into the carburettor intake, lift the air valve, and screw the jet until its edge is just flush with the bridge. Then screw it down by two turns.

3 Screw the adjusting screw down by two turns.

4 Top-up the dashpot, refit the hydraulic damper. Check that the air valve falls freely on to the bridge when lifted and released. If it does not, see "Centralizing the Jet" on page 63.

5 Start the engine, run it until it has regained its normal temperature and then adjust the throttle stop-screw or screws to give smooth idling at a speed of 600–650 r.p.m. There should be an equal hiss from the intakes of both carburettors when twin carburettors are fitted. *This is very important.* If necessary, re-synchronize the carburettors as described in the next section.

6 If the exhaust note is irregular, lift the air valve of the carburettor (or one carburettor of a twin installation) a very small amount—*not exceeding $\frac{1}{32}$ in.*—with the tip of a penknife blade or a thin screwdriver. If the engine speed rises appreciably, the mixture supplied by that carburettor is too rich. If the engine stops, the mixture is too weak. When each carburettor if a twin installation is properly adjusted, the engine speed will either remain constant or will fall very slightly when each air valve is lifted.

Special Notes

The best way to match the idling speeds of twin carburettors is to use one of the several types of air-flow meters that are sold by accessory shops.

Alternatively, hold one end of a length of plastic tubing at the same spot in each carburettor and listen to the hiss.

It is essential not to set the mixture strength when a carburettor is overheated—for example, after the car has been standing for some time with the engine hot and the bonnet closed. There is a risk that the mixture will be set too weak. As already mentioned, this may damage the valves.

If satisfactory idling cannot be obtained when the adjusting screw is within half-a-turn up or down from the starting position (*see* **2** and **3** above), check that the shoulder on the needle is flush with the base of the air-valve piston and that the securing screw is tight. *See* Carburettor Servicing on page 56.

To synchronize twin Zenith-Stromberg carburettors:

If the synchronization of the carburettors has been upset—for example, when they have been removed from the engine—the two throttles must be re-synchronized. To do this:

1 Loosen the most accessible clamping bolt on the throttle-spindle couplings.
2 Unscrew each throttle stop-screw to allow the throttle to close completely.
3 Screw in each throttle stop-screw until its tip just nips a 0·002-in. (0·05-mm) feeler-gauge blade against the stop-lever on the throttle spindle. From this point, rotate the stop-screws two complete turns clockwise.
4 This setting provides the basis from which final very careful adjustment of each screw can be made, in conjunction with the mixture adjustments described earlier, to provide even, regular idling.
5 Tighten the spindle clamp screw.

Special Notes

It will be appreciated that although each throttle stop-screw must normally be rotated by the same amount in order to keep the two carburettors in step, slight difference in efficiency between the individual cylinders, the valve gear, sparking plugs and induction and exhaust tracts, usually mean that the settings on each carburettor for best results are not exactly the same.

Fig. 21. Starting carburettor adjuster on a Zenith-Stromberg
1, stop pin. 2, normal position. 3, position for very cold weather

Adjusting the Cold-starting Setting—Stromberg 150CDS Carburettor.
The spring-loaded stop pin (shown in Fig. 21) is normally set fully "in," with the pin vertical, for all temperatures down to −18°C. In very cold

climates, a richer mixture can be obtained by turning the pin to the horizontal position so that it engages with the groove in the housing.

CARBURETTOR SERVICING

Modern carburettors are relatively trouble-free units—which is probably why they are often neglected until, after thousands of miles of uncomplaining service, they eventually give trouble—usually owing to the accumulation of water or fine sediment in the float chamber, which blocks the jets or the passages which feed them.

The Zenith-Stromberg types are less liable to this trouble, owing to the fact that they have only one large-diameter jet which is metered by a continually moving needle, but the Zenith static carburettors are more susceptible to blockage and repay thorough cleaning and checking at 12,000-miles intervals. This does not mean, however, that the Zenith-Stromberg design needs no attention; again, a thorough 12,000-miles check will help to forestall trouble.

Before describing the work on the various types of carburettor, an important word of warning must be given: *Never dismantle a carburettor when the engine is hot, owing to the risk of fire—and, of course, do not smoke while working on the carburettor.*

12-1: Servicing Zenith Static Carburettors

Dismantling the Zenith IV and IZ carburettors sufficiently to check and clean the jets, acceleration pump, economy device, float and float needle valve is quite straightforward. It is not necessary to strip the carburettor completely during normal servicing, although the "exploded" drawings show the relationship of all the parts. It must be emphasized that we are dealing here only with normal cleaning and inspection. More complicated items such as water-heated automatic choke mechanism, when fitted, should not be dismantled by a novice. Leave this sort of job to your Vauxhall dealer.

The jets should be cleaned by washing them in petrol and blowing through them in the reverse direction to the normal flow of fuel. Never be tempted to probe them with wire. They are calibrated to very fine limits and engine performance and economy will suffer if the drillings are altered or even scratched. The jets are clearly numbered—the greater the number, the larger the jet.

After cleaning the jets the slow-running adjustments should, if necessary, be reset as described on pages 50–53.

To check and clean Zenith 30IZ and IZE carburettors:

1 If blockage of the acceleration pump jet is suspected (this will cause a "flat spot" during acceleration) remove the air cleaner, look into the carburettor air intake, and sharply open the throttle. Petrol should spurt from the jet into the air intake. If it does not, it will be

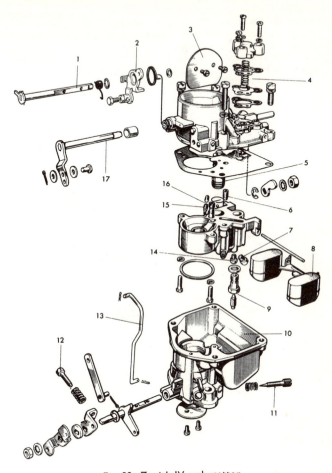

Fig. 22. Zenith IV carburettor

1, choke spindle. 2, choke control lever. 3, choke flap. 4, economy valve assembly. 5, acceleration pump piston. 6, idling jet. 7, main jet. 8, float. 9, float needle valve. 10, float chamber. 11, idling mixture adjusting screw. 12, throttle stop screw. 13, throttle-choke interconnecting rod. 14, compensating jet. 15, pump jet. 16, pump discharge valve. 17, pump operating spindle and lever

necessary to dismantle the carburettor to gain access to the jet, as described below.

2 Remove the cover from the carburettor body.

3 Lift out the pump jet and blow through it to remove any obstruction.

4 Replace the pump jet, *and holding it in position*, open the throttle sharply. If the petrol still fails to spurt from the jet, the pump is faulty. Usually the trouble is a cracked or perforated diaphragm. *Do not operate the throttle without the pump jet in position.*

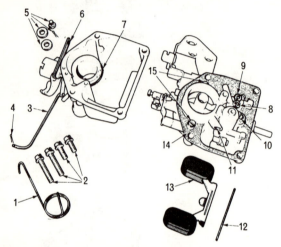

Fig. 23. Float, float chamber and jets of Zenith IV series carburettors

1, throttle return spring. 2, top cover retaining screws and lock-washer. 3, throttle and choke interconnecting rod. 4, split pin—throttle and choke interconnecting rod. 5, pin and washers—acceleration pump operating link. 6, acceleration pump operating link. 7, sealing ring. 8, main jet. 9, compensating jet. 10, needle valve assembly. 11, plug—remove for access to acceleration pump jet. 12, float hinge pin. 13, float. 14, top cover gasket. 15, emulsion block retaining screws

5 Assuming that the acceleration pump is satisfactory, remove the float and lever assembly, taking care not to lose the float pivot pin.

6 Drain the carburettor by removing the hexagon plug from the end of the float chamber. Place a cloth under the float chamber to soak up the petrol.

7 Remove and clean the main jet, air correction and emulsion tube assembly and slow-running jet. All of these can be identified in the illustration (Fig. 24).

8 Check the gasket fitted between the cover and the carburettor body, and renew it if necessary. *This gasket is vital to the correct operation of the carburettor.*

9 Replace the top cover. Open the choke flap before fitting the cover to ensure the correct positioning of the choke linkage.

10 Replace the air cleaner.

Special Notes

The stroke of the acceleration pump on 30IZ carburettors is adjustable for summer or winter use. The pump operating rod should be inserted in the lower hole in the summer. In winter it should be in the upper hole.

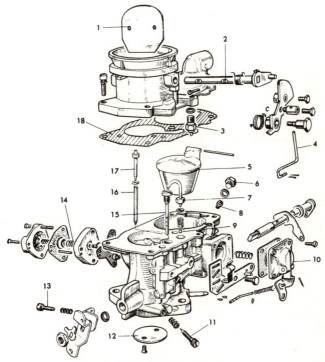

Fig. 24. Zenith IZ carburettor

1, choke flap. 2, choke spindle. 3, float needle valve. 4, throttle-choke interconnecting rod. 5, float. 6, main jet plug. 7, pump injector. 8, main jet. 9, acceleration pump ball valve. 10, acceleration pump cover. 11, idling mixture adjusting screw. 12, throttle plate. 13, throttle stop screw. 14, economy valve assembly. 15, emulsion tube and correction jet. 16, idling jet filter. 17, idling jet. 18, gasket

To check and clean Zenith 36IV, IVE, IVT and IVET carburettors:

1 Remove the air cleaner, disconnect the choke control, the throttle control, and the petrol feed pipe.

2 Remove the split-pin from the throttle and choke interconnecting rod, and pull out the rod.

3 Disconnect the acceleration pump operating link from the throttle lever.

4 Remove the throttle return spring, noting in which two slots the short leg of the spring is positioned.

5 Remove the top cover.

6 Slide out the float hinge pin, remove the float and lift out the needle valve.

7 Remove the pump discharge jet and the main and compensating jets.

8 Remove the emulsion block, with the acceleration pump piston, and take out the slow-running jet and the pump check valve. *Do not try to remove the pump inlet ball valve and its circlip from the bottom of the pump bore.*

9 When reassembling the carburettor, the following points are important —Renew the gasket if it is not in perfect condition. When refitting the emulsion block to the top cover, the acceleration pump operating lever must point towards the centre line of the top cover. The acceleration pump link pin must be inserted into the correct hole in the lever (*see* below). The two long cover retaining screws fit the two holes with the deepest bosses. The open end of the short leg of the throttle return spring should point towards the carburettor when the throttle is in the closed position.

Special Notes

Although two holes are provided in the acceleration pump spindle lever on IVT carburettors, the pump linkage connecting pin should always be assembled to the upper hole on 1800 engines and in the lower hole on 1,256 c.c. engines.

12-1 (contd.): Servicing Zenith-Stromberg Carburettors

The Stromberg 150CDS carburettor is shown in Fig. 25. The jet is in the form of a metal tube, fed with fuel from the float chamber through holes near its base. The effective size of the opening at the top of the jet, through which fuel is sprayed into the air which is drawn through the carburettor into the engine is controlled by a tapered needle, clamped in the base of a piston or air valve which rises and falls as the airflow varies with changes in the engine speed and the throttle opening. The varying vacuum acts on a rubber diaphragm which is clamped to the air valve, the space between the diaphragm and the top cover of the carburettor forming a chamber which is subject, through a drilling in the air valve, to the fluctuating suction in the carburettor throat.

Since the needle controls the flow of petrol, and the piston varies the size of the air passage in the carburettor as it rises and falls, the correct petrol/air mixture is maintained under all running conditions.

The mixture strength can be altered over the whole range of running, if necessary, simply by substituting a needle that has a different taper; and the amount of petrol in the idling mixture (when the piston is at its lowest position) can be controlled by raising or lowering the jet in relation to the needle.

The very rich mixture which is needed to start a cold engine is provided by a separate starting carburettor on the side of the main carburettor. When a hand-operated "choke" control is pulled out, a disc valve is rotated in the starting carburettor, to provide additional fuel, and at the same time the throttle is opened slightly by a cam on the disc valve spindle.

When an automatic choke is fitted, the richness of the starting mixture is controlled by a tapered needle, and the fast-idling speed by a stepped cam. A bi-metal coiled spring, which is influenced by the temperature of the water passing through the starting carburettor, controls both these actions.

The carburettor metering needle which is fitted as standard (as the result of extensive tests) will normally give the best performance and fuel economy. Carburettor tuning is always to some extent a compromise, however, and if the car is usually operated at a high altitude, a needle that gives a weaker mixture than normal may be justified. On the other hand, if the engine is tuned for increased performance, a slightly richer needle may be needed. Consult your local Vauxhall dealer if you feel that a change of needle is needed to suit abnormal running conditions.

The only routine maintenance required is occasional topping-up of the small oil-well in the upper part of the suction chamber and an occasional check on the adjustment of the slow-running strength and idling speed. At comparatively long intervals—say, once every 10,000 miles or yearly— the suction chamber and the piston should be cleaned and the diaphragm should be checked for cracks or pin-holes as described below.

To inspect the diaphragm, piston and needle:

One of the most likely causes of carburation troubles with a Stromberg carburettor is a cracked or perforated diaphragm. It can be inspected, and renewed if necessary, without removing the carburettor from the engine. At the same time, the piston and needle can be checked and cleaned.

1 Remove the depression cover from the top of the carburettor, after taking out the screws.
2 Lift out the piston and detach the diaphragm by removing the screws that clamp the retaining ring.
3 Fit a new diaphragm, if necessary, making sure that the locating tabs

on its rim fit into the recesses in the carburettor body and in the upper end of the air-valve piston.

4 Before replacing the piston, make sure that the shoulder on the needle is just flush with the base of the piston, and that the needle-locking screw is tight. If the needle is bent it must, of course, be renewed.

Special Notes

The diaphragm retaining-ring must be replaced very carefully, It is easy to displace the diaphragm from its correct position on the air-valve piston.

The piston-return spring must not be stretched or shortened. It has a critical effect on the mixture strength at all engine speeds.

To check the float-chamber level:

If it is not possible to obtain smooth idling after carrying out the adjustments described earlier, the trouble may be to an incorrect petrol-level in the float chamber of the carburettor or carburettors.

To check the level:

1 Remove the carburettor from the engine.
2 Take off the float chamber and invert the carburettor so that the highest point of the float above the face of the main body can be measured when the needle valve is resting on its seating. The correct height is 16 mm.
3 If necessary, reset the level of the float by carefully bending the tag that makes contact with the end of the needle valve. Alternatively, the addition of a thin fibre washer beneath the needle-valve seating will effectively lower the petrol-level and will cure symptoms of over-richness caused by slight wear on the valve and seating.
4 If correct setting of the float does not cure over-richness or flooding, the wisest plan is to renew the needle-valve assembly in each carburettor. These are not expensive items and do not have an unlimited life. It is often advised that they should be renewed after about 20,000 miles.

To centralize the jet:

Difficult starting and other carburettor troubles can be caused by a sticking air valve. Check for this fault by lifting the valve with the spring-loaded pin beneath the suction-chamber housing and allowing it to fall. If the valve does not fall freely, with an audible click, it is a straightforward matter to remove it and clean the sliding portion and the bore in which it works. Use only petrol or paraffin. Do not lubricate the valve and don't be tempted to use emery cloth or metal polish to brighten it up, as the clearance between the valve and the bore is fairly critical.

If, on reassembly, the valve still does not fall freely, either the needle may be bent or the jet may be out-of-centre. In either case, the needle will be rubbing against the side of the bore of the jet. The remedy, if the carburettor is not of the emission-controlled type, is to fit a new needle, with its shoulder flush with the lower face of the air valve and to re-centralize the jet. Some emission-controlled carburettors, however, have spring-loaded needles and in these cases there is intentional light

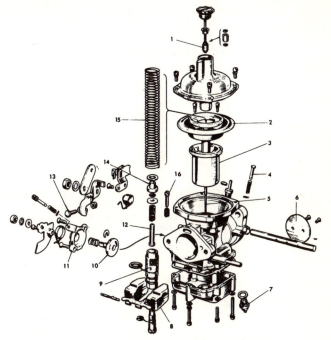

Fig. 25. Zenith-Stromberg 150 CDS carburettor

1, air valve damper piston. 2, diaphragm. 3, air valve piston. 4, test pin. 5, needle. 6, throttle plate. 7, float needle valve. 8, float. 9, jet sleeve. 10, starter disc. 11, starter housing. 12, jet. 13, throttle stop screw. 14, jet bush. 15, spring. 16, throttle stop screw

rubbing contact between the needle and the jet in order to improve the regulation of the mixture strength under all running conditions. When this type of needle is fitted, centralizing the jet is not required.

To centralize the jet in a fixed-needle carburettor:

1 Lift the air valve and screw-up the jet adjusting-nut until the jet is slightly above the level of the bridge.

2 Slacken the hexagon at the base of the jet-bush screw. Half-a-turn should be sufficient to free the bush and allow the jet to centralize itself around the needle when the air valve is allowed to fall.

3 Carefully tighten the hexagon, while checking that the needle is still free, as indicated by a sharp click when the base of the air valve strikes the bridge.

4 After this adjustment the idling settings must be restored as described earlier.

CARBURETTOR FAULT-TRACING

Difficult starting, heavy fuel consumption, misfiring and loss of power are often blamed on the carburettor, when the trouble is in fact due to some other fault, or to a combination of ignition and mechanical engine faults. When discussing carburettor faults, therefore, it must be assumed that the carburettor idling adjustments are correct (very important with Stromberg carburettors) and that preliminary checks for ignition and mechanical faults have been carried out. The charts in Chapter 12 may help to isolate the trouble.

Difficult Starting

1 Check the adjustment of the starting-mixture control and the fast-idle setting, and make sure that the jet piston is not sticking.

2 Verify that petrol is reaching the float chamber; the needle valve may be sticking or the float may be incorrectly adjusted, giving a very low fuel-level, which starves the jet.

Excessive Fuel Consumption

1 Check for leakage of petrol from the jet or unions, flooding, or too high a petrol-level in the float chamber.

2 As mentioned above, the carburettor is often blamed for heavy consumption when the trouble is due to poor engine condition. Don't overlook the possibility of over-retarded ignition timing. Binding brakes are another common cause.

Special Notes

Short journeys and town driving will increase the petrol consumption quite appreciably. The average figure given in Chapter 1 is generally stated by car manufacturers in terms of country running over give-and-take roads with normal loads at modest speeds. The consumption will increase, of course, when the car is driven hard.

Lack of Power, Misfiring, Poor Acceleration, Low Top Speed

1 Top-up the piston-damper chamber with the correct grade of oil.

2 Check for a sticking carburettor piston or a perforated diaphragm.

3 Check for fuel starvation caused by a low float-chamber fuel-level or a faulty petrol pump.
4 Check for ignition and mechanical faults—*see* Chapter 12.

THE PETROL PUMP

The A.C. mechanical pump (Figs. 17 and 18) is operated by a rocker arm which pulls a diaphragm downwards against spring pressure, drawing the petrol through the filter and past the flange of an inlet valve into the pumping chamber above the diaphragm. When the arm moves in the opposite direction, a spring raises the diaphragm and forces the petrol through the outlet valve into the outlet union and so, through the feed pipe, to the carburettor.

When the carburettor float-chamber is full, the float-operated needle valve closes and the pressure that is built-up in the pumping-chamber above the diaphragm keeps the diaphragm in its lower position against the pressure of the spring. The outer end of the rocker arm moves freely up and down and delivery ceases until the petrol-level in the float chamber falls and the needle valve opens.

The pump requires no maintenance except for occasional cleaning of the filter (*see* page 48). The sealing ring between the top cover and the pump body must be in good condition, since an air leak past the flange of the cover will put the pump out of action.

A pump which gives trouble is best replaced by a service-exchange unit. If fuel starvation is suspected:

1 Disconnect the carburettor-end of the fuel delivery pipe, place it in a suitable container and rotate the engine with the low-tension wire disconnected from the ignition coil, to prevent the engine starting. Regular spurts of fuel should flow from the pipe. *Be careful not to allow any sparking from the disconnected wire and do not smoke while making the test.*
2 If fuel is being delivered, check the carburettor needle valve and needle seating. The needle may be stuck or the fuel passage obstructed.
3 If the fuel contains air bubbles, check the condition of the filter-cover gasket and the tightness of the retaining screw. The gasket must be in good condition, as mentioned earlier.
4 If the pump seems to be in order, there must be an air leak in the pipe from the fuel tank to the pump.
5 If there is no fuel flow, and no air bubbles appear, the pump is probably faulty and should be replaced.

8 The clutch, gearbox and rear axle

THE drive is taken from the engine to the rear wheels by the clutch, gearbox or automatic transmission, propeller shaft and the rear axle. Attention to these items is normally confined to lubrication at the intervals specified in the maintenance schedule, when the checks described in this chapter should also be carried out.

The Clutch. Some beginners have a habit of driving with the left foot resting on the clutch pedal. This is a bad practice; even light pressure, if applied continuously, will cause unnecessary wear of the clutch-release bearing—that is, the bearing that transfers the thrust from the clutch pedal to the clutch-release fingers of the pressure plate—leading to noisy operation and excessive clutch-pedal travel. The same fault will occur if the clutch is slipped to avoid changing to a lower gear when the engine is overloaded. Wear on the friction linings will eventually cause persistent clutch-slip, and a clutch overhaul, which is a moderately expensive job, will then be needed.

There should be a free movement of $\frac{1}{2}$–$\frac{3}{4}$ in. at the clutch pedal, before the weight of the clutch spring is felt. This will gradually decrease as the clutch friction-lining wears, and occasional adjustment to the length of the clutch-operating cable will therefore be needed, as described below.

6-11: Adjusting the Clutch Operating Cable

If a free movement of $\frac{1}{2}$–$\frac{3}{4}$ in. (13–19 mm) does not exist at the clutch pedal, the clutch-operating cable should be adjusted at the lower end, where it is connected to the clutch-operating lever (Fig. 27).

1 Tighten the clutch cable adjusting nut until the clutch release bearing is just nipped by the operating lever. This can be checked by inserting a finger through the unused clutch fork slot in the housing and spinning the bearing while tightening the adjusting nut.
2 Screw the lock-nut back from the adjusting nut to the extent of $\frac{1}{4}$ in. (6 mm) for push-rod engines, and $\frac{3}{16}$ in. (5 mm) for overhead-camshaft units.
3 Screw the adjusting nut back until it contacts the lock-nut and then lock the two together.

Special Notes

The release lever and the release bearing are shown in Fig. 26. The reason for rotating the bearing while carrying out adjustment is that otherwise it is difficult to judge just when the bearing begins to apply pressure to the fingers of the diaphragm spring, which offer only a very low resistance during the first part of the clutch pedal travel.

The Gearbox. A manual gearbox needs no attention, other than checking the oil-level during routine servicing and topping-up if necessary with the grade of oil specified in Chapter 1. Any oil leaks will be obvious while this is being done. If they are serious, ask your dealer for advice.

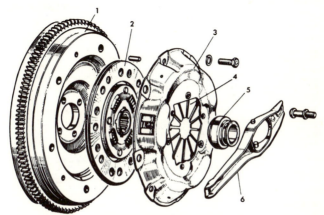

Fig. 26. The clutch components

1, flywheel. 2, clutch centre plate. 3, clutch cover assembly. 4, diaphragm spring. 5, release bearing, 6, operating lever

When trouble develops in the gearbox, considerable experience is needed to diagnose it with any degree of certainty. Excessive noise, or a tendency to jump out of gear, are usually caused by the cumulative effect of wear at a number of points, over a large mileage. Piecemeal replacements are seldom effective for very long; usually the most economical course is to fit a reconditioned gearbox.

6-12: Checking the Gearbox Oil Level

A combined oil-level and filler plug is provided on the left-hand side of the gearbox. To inject the oil, it will be necessary to use a flexible-tube extension on the spout of an oil-can, or one of the special Castrol Handi-Pack dispensers filled with gear oil (the correct grade is given in Chapter 1). The plug can be reached from beneath the car.

1 With the car on a level surface, unscrew the plug, after cleaning the area around it.

2 If oil does not flow from the opening, inject oil until it overflows and allow times for the surplus oil to run out before replacing the filler plugs.

The Automatic Transmission. The adjustment of the selector linkage and the other controls of an automatic transmission should not be disturbed without good reason, as readjustment calls for considerable care to ensure satisfactory gear selection and the correct timing of the gearchanges. Also, let your dealer change the fluid every 24,000 miles, clean the filter, and adjust the low band servo. Adjustment of the inhibitor switch, prevents the starter being operated except when the transmission selector is at N or P, is dealt with in Chapter 11.

Otherwise, servicing is confined to checking the fluid level at 6,000-miles intervals.

6-12: Checking the Fluid Level in the Automatic Transmission

The filler-tube and dipstick for the automatic transmission are in the engine compartment, just in front of the bulkhead.

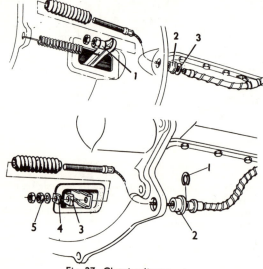

Fig. 27. Clutch adjustment

On push-rod engines (above), a ball-type adjusting nut, 1, is used. A rubber insulator, 2, and circular washer, 3, are fitted at the end of the cable. On overhead-camshaft engines (below), a horseshoe washer, 1, is used with the insulator, 2. There is also an insulator, 3, and a pressure pad, 4, between the end of the cable and the adjusting nut, 5

To check the fluid level:

1 With the car on a level surface *and the engine and transmission at the normal running temperature* select "P" and allow the engine to idle for two minutes.
2 With the engine still idling, withdraw the dipstick, wipe it on clean, non-fluffy cloth or paper, re-insert it and withdraw it immediately.
3 If necessary, add fluid to bring the level up to the "Full" mark.

Special Notes

Scrupulous cleanliness is essential when checking the level or topping-up. Use only special automatic transmission fluid, obtainable from your dealer. Keep the underside of the transmission free from mud—especially the ventilator grilles. Otherwise the fluid may overheat.

The Propeller Shaft. The universal joints that connect the propeller shaft to the gearbox and rear axle are fitted with needle-roller bearings which are lubricated during assembly and usually have a very long life. The sliding, splined section of the front joint is lubricated automatically from the gearbox.

Check the tightness of the flange bolts at each end of the shaft during routine servicing. Also test the joints for wear by attempting to raise and lower the shaft at each end. Loose flange bolts and worn bearings can cause pronounced transmission vibration at higher road-speeds and a knock when accelerating, decelerating and starting from a standstill.

When looseness eventually develops in the bearings (usually after a very large mileage) the complete assembly of propeller shaft and joints should be renewed.

The Rear Axle. The teeth of the hypoid gears in the back axle are subject to very high stresses and require an "extreme-pressure" lubricating oil of the type specified in Chapter 1, which prevents breakdown of the oil film. The oil level should be checked and topped-up at regular intervals. There is no need to drain and refill the axle—except, of course, during an overhaul.

As with the other transmission components, rear-axle repairs are not normally within the scope of the do-it-yourself owner.

In the larger garages, assembly of the final-drive and differential gears is usually entrusted to a man who specializes in this particular type of job. Smaller concerns generally prefer to fit a reconditioned assembly which requires no further adjustment.

6-13: Checking the Rear Axle Oil Level

The combined filler and level plug is in the rear face of the axle casing. As in the case of the gearbox, a flexible extension for the oil-can or a

Castrol Handi-Pack filled with gear oil will make the job of topping-up much easier. The car must be on a level surface.

1 Wipe the area around the plug and unscrew the plug.
2 If oil does not flow out, inject a small quantity and allow the overflow to cease before refitting the plug.

9 The braking system

EITHER Girling or Lockheed hydraulic brakes may be fitted, at the front or rear. The Standard and de Luxe Viva models have drum brakes on all four wheels, whereas the other Vivas and the Magnums have drum brakes at the rear and disc brakes on the front wheels. A vacuum servo is fitted to disc-braked cars to reduce the effort required at the brake pedal.

Separate front and rear hydraulic circuits ensure that all braking power will not be lost if fluid should leak from the front or the rear brakes or pipelines.

For the benefit of the novice it should perhaps be explained that in an hydraulic braking system, fluid pressure is generated in a master cylinder when the brake pedal is depressed. This pressure is transmitted through pipelines to pistons in "slave" cylinders which operate the front and rear brakes. When the front wheels are fitted with disc brakes, the hydraulic pistons force steel pads, faced with friction material, against the sides of a steel disc which is attached to the wheel hub. In the case of drum brakes the brake cylinders are mounted on the stationary backplate of each brake and the pistons force the brake shoes, which are lined with special friction material, into contact with the rotating drums.

Disc brakes call for higher operating pressures than drum brakes (owing to the relatively small area of friction pad that is pressed against the disc), so a vacuum-servo is provided as standard to reduce the effort required at the brake pedal, when disc brakes are fitted. The servo piston, operated by the partial vacuum which exists in the inlet manifold of the engine, acts on the hydraulic piston in the master cylinder and boosts the pressure in the brake lines by a ratio of about 2:1.

Brake Servicing. The routine maintenance required by the braking system is summarized in the maintenance schedule. The periodical checks on the fluid level, and on the condition of the brake linings or friction pads, are particularly important from the safety aspect. The need to change the brake fluid after about two years of service, and to renew the rubber hoses, pistons and seals in the system after 36,000 miles (60,000 km) or three years, must not be forgotten. These are also essential safety precautions.

W-6, 6-14: Checking the Level in the Brake-fluid Reservoir

The brake-fluid level should be checked at regular intervals. A weekly check takes little time and is a wise precaution.

1 Wipe the cap of the brake-fluid reservoir (mounted on the engine bulkhead or in the brake servo) and unscrew it. Do not place the cap on the bodywork, as the fluid acts as a fairly efficient paint stripper!

2 Top-up the fluid-level, if necessary, to within about $\frac{1}{2}$ in. of the top of the reservoir.

3 Replace the cap and check the paintwork for any drips of brake fluid.

Special Notes

Checking the fluid level is primarily a precaution, but a vital one.

Topping-up should be required only at fairly long intervals, although it is normal for the level in the brake master cylinder of cars fitted with disc brakes to fall as the friction pads wear.

If the level of the fluid in the reservoir has dropped appreciably, check the pipelines and operating cylinders for any signs of leakage. If slight leakage has occurred—say, from a slack union—air may have entered the system, giving the pedal a characteristically "spongy" feel. The method of eliminating the air from the system is described under "Bleeding the Brakes."

Check that the air-vent hole in the filler cap of the reservoir is clear. If this is choked there is a risk of the brakes dragging.

Finally, never store brake fluid in an unsealed container, or for long periods in a partly-filled tin. It quickly absorbs moisture from the air and this can be dangerous if the heat generated by the brakes causes steam bubbles to form in the wheel cylinders. It is better to buy small quantities of fluid at reasonably frequent intervals.

6-14: Brakes—Preventive Check

1 Remove the drums from drum brakes (*see* "Relining the Brakes"), blow out the dust, check the condition of the linings and adjust the brakes after the drums have been refitted.

2 Check the condition of the brake friction pads and discs when disc brakes are fitted. These can be examined when the front wheels have been removed. If the thickness of the pads has been reduced to $\frac{1}{8}$ in. or if they are unlikely to last until the next service, fit new pads (*see* "Fitting New Friction Pads to Disc Brakes"). If the discs are badly scored they should be renewed by a dealer.

If one pad in a calliper is more worn than the other, there is no objection to changing the pads around in order to equalize the wear and to obtain a longer life from the pair, but they will take a few hundred miles to bed-in.

3 Check the brake pipes and hoses for any signs of leakage or damage,

and—most important—for signs of rusting on the steel pipes, which can start within two years, and which could result in complete brake failure. The handbrake compensator and cable guides should be lubricated at this mileage.

6-14: Brake Adjustment

Front disc brakes are self-adjusting and require no attention during the life of the friction pads, provided that the checks described in this chapter are carried out at specified intervals. The Lockheed rear brakes fitted to some models are also self-adjusting, a fine-toothed ratchet plate in each brake mechanism compensating for wear whenever the brakes are applied and maintaining the correct shoe-to-drum clearance.

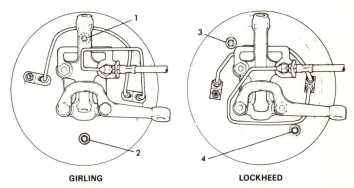

GIRLING   **LOCKHEED**

Fig. 28. Girling and Lockheed front drum brake

The adjusters, 1–4, are differently placed on Girling and Lockheed drum-type front brakes. On the rear brakes the single adjuster is at the 12 o'clock, 1 o'clock or 7 o'clock position

Other types of Girling and Lockheed drum brakes, however, will require adjustment from time to time, the need for this being indicated when the brake pedal travel exceeds about $2\frac{3}{4}$ in. (70 mm) when a force of 70 pounds is applied to the pedal—that is, a fairly heavy foot pressure. Don't postpone adjustment until the pedal nearly goes down to the floor. When the brakes are servo-assisted, the engine must not be running while making this test and the vacuum servo should be exhausted by applying the brakes several times until the pedal feels "hard."

To adjust the brakes:

1 Chock one wheel, release the handbrake and jack up a wheel on the opposite side of the car. Spin the wheel to make sure that it is running freely and then locate the squared adjuster spindle or spindles on the

brake backplate. There are two spindles on a front brake, Fig. 28 shows their positions on Girling and Lockheed brakes. Each rear brake has only a single adjusting spindle, roughly at the 12 o'clock," "1 o'clock," or "7 o'clock" position when the backplate is viewed from the inner side of the wheel.

2 Using a special brake adjusting spanner, turn each adjuster, on Girling brakes, clockwise, as viewed from the inside of the wheel, until the drum is locked. Then turn the adjuster back until the drum is just free. On Lockheed brakes both the adjusters must be rotated in the forward direction of rotation of the wheel—that is, clockwise on the left-hand side and anti-clockwise on the right-hand side.

3 Spin the wheel and apply and release the foot brake. Check that the adjustment is still correct.

4 Repeat the adjustment on the other brakes. Rotate the adjusters as described for the front brakes.

Special Notes

It is only too easy to round-off the corners of the adjusting spindles if an ordinary open spanner is used. A suitable tool (VR102) can be obtained from Vauxhall dealers, and special brake adjusting spanners can also be bought from accessory shops.

The spindles often tend to become partly-seized and it is as well to dose them with penetrating oil before beginning work.

The brake drum usually tends to rub against the shoe at one point during rotation. Drums always seem to warp to some extent in service and light rubbing at one point must be accepted if, to cure it completely, it would be necessary to back-off the adjustment to such an extent as to cause excessive brake pedal travel.

6-14: Handbrake Adjustment

Normally, correct adjustment of the rear-brake shoes will eliminate any excessive free movement on the handbrake lever. In time, however, the handbrake cable will stretch and it will be necessary to take up the slack by shortening the cable. Be careful not to adjust the cable too tightly, as this will prevent the automatic adjuster working.

1 Chock the front wheels securely and jack-up and support the rear of the car.

2 Release the handbrake fully and then pull the lever up by one notch. If the rear end of the brake cable is attached to a yoke, through which the cable which operates the rear brake levers passes, slacken the lock-nut and turn the adjusting sleeve to take up slackness in the cables without causing the rear brake shoes to rub. Tighten the lock-nut. When the front handbrake cable is connected to an equalizer, pivoted on a mounting bracket on the rear axle and connected to the brake operating levers by rods or cables, the length of the front cable can

be adjusted by slackening the lock-nut, removing the pin which links the clevis or fork to the equalizer and screwing the fork along the threaded rod. When refitting the pin, use a new split-pin. Tighten the lock-nut firmly.

3 If the full range of adjustment is taken up on a yoke-type linkage without removing all the slackness in the cables, unscrew the adjuster and disconnect the forks which attach the ends of the transverse cable to the operating levers on the rear brakes. Transfer the pins to the inner holes in the forks, with their heads against the slots in the forks. Fit new split-pins. On Girling brakes, the brake shoe lever has two holes and the clevis pin must be assembled in the hole at the end of the lever.

4 Check that the operating levers on the brake backplates are fully back on their stops.

Bleeding the Brakes

If, as mentioned earlier, the level of the fluid in the reservoir is allowed to fall too low, or if a pipeline union is disconnected or slackens-off, air will enter the braking system, and to eliminate it you will have to "bleed" the brakes. This is *not* a normal routine job.

A bleed nipple, which incorporates a ball valve, will be found on the backplate of each front brake, or on each disc-brake calliper (*see* Figs. 30 and 31), and also on the right-hand rear-brake backplate. The left-hand rear brake has no nipple. It is bled simultaneously with the right-hand brake. Some export models have a brake-failure warning light on the instrument panel. The switch which controls this light is operated by a small piston in the brake master cylinder which is moved from its central position when pressure is lost in the front or rear brake pipelines. Since opening a bleed valve has the same effect as, say, a fractured pipeline or a disconnected union in causing an unbalanced pressure in the system, the switch will operate and the lamp will light.

Normally, bleeding the brakes is a two-man job—one to open and close the bleed screw and to watch for air bubbles in the fluid which is pumped out, and the other to operate the brake pedal and to top-up the master cylinder as required.

Several ingenious devices are available which enable the job to be carried out single-handed, however, and it is as well to look-over the selection at your local accessory shop before deciding to tackle the job the hard way.

If no easy-bleeding device is used:

1 Attach a rubber or transparent plastic tube to the nipple on the left-hand front wheel in the case of a right-hand drive car, or the right-hand front wheel on a left-hand drive model. Pass the tube through a box or ring spanner that fits the hexagon on the nipple. Submerge the free end of the tube in a little brake fluid in a clean glass jar.

2 If a servo is fitted, pump the brake pedal several times to exhaust the vacuum in the servo system.

3 Open the bleed screw one complete turn. Your assistant should now depress the brake pedal with a slow, full stroke, followed by two or three short rapid strokes, and then allow it to return unassisted. Top-up the fluid level in the master cylinder reservoir with the fresh fluid. Repeat the pumping strokes after about 5 seconds.

4 Watch the flow of liquid into the jar and continue pumping until air bubbles cease. Tighten the bleed screw while the pedal is held down fully. *Do not overtighten the screw.*

5 Repeat this operation on the other brakes, first with the remaining front wheel and following with the right-hand rear wheel.

24-1: Flushing the System

After two years or about 24,000 miles (40,000 km) or when a vehicle has been laid-up for some considerable time, the fluid in the system may become thick or gummy. The system should then be drained, flushed and refilled:

1 Pump out all fluid through the bleeder screw of each wheel cylinder in turn, as described above, and discard it.

2 Fill the reservoir with methylated spirit and flush the system by pumping as before. The supply tank should be replenished until at least a quart of spirit has passed through each wheel cylinder.

3 Finally, pump the reservoir dry, refill with clean brake fluid and "bleed" the system.

Special Notes

If the fluid has been contaminated by the use of mineral oil, all the hydraulic units, including the pipelines, should be dismantled and thoroughly cleaned and all rubber parts, including flexible hoses, should be replaced. If an oil has been used, this will separate out when the fluid has been allowed to stand for an hour or two in a glass jar; the layers of different fluid can then be seen. The contaminated fluid should be discarded immediately to avoid it being accidentally re-used.

Relining the Brakes

Dismantling drum brakes is quite straightforward:

1 Jack-up the car and remove the wheel. Make sure that the handbrake is fully off.

2 Remove the drum, after taking out the securing screw.

3 Remove the brake-shoe steady pins and springs.

4 Remove the shoes and pull-off springs by levering the tip of one shoe away from the fixed stop on the backplate. The shoes can then be collapsed together, allowing the pull-off springs to be unhooked and

the shoes to be removed. Make a note of how the pull-off springs are fitted to the shoes. On Girling front brakes, only the longer end of the shoe return spring is attached to the shoe, the other end being anchored to the backplate. On Lockheed brakes, both ends of the spring are hooked into the shoes, with the longer hooked end next to the brake adjuster. Notice also that Lockheed rear brakes have a fixed hydraulic cylinder with two opposed pistons and a strut attached to the handbrake lever, whereas on Girling brakes a "floating" operating cylinder, free to move slightly on the back-plate and having only one piston, is used. Correct identification of the braking system fitted is, of course, essential if any new parts are needed.

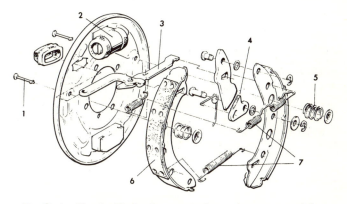

Fig. 29. Lockheed self-adjusting rear brake used on some models

1, shoe steady pin. 2, operating cylinder. 3, handbrake-operated lever. 4, self-adjuster ratchet. 5, shoe steady spring. 6, friction lining on shoe. 7, pull-off springs

5 Clean the backplate thoroughly with paraffin. Make sure that the operating cylinder can slide on the backplate, to centralize the shoes, and that the lever operated by the handbrake is not stiff or seized-up. A thorough clean-up and soaking with penetrating oil (keep this away from the rubber parts) will usually free the components. If the tip of the lever engaging with the adjusting nut is worn, a complete new lever mechanism must be fitted. Lubricate all the parts except the tip of the lever and the teeth of the adjusting nut with a light smear of special brake grease. Keep the grease away from the linings.

6 Before refitting the shoes, withdraw the ratchet-wheel assembly of the automatic adjuster from the lever. Make sure that the toothed wheel is not binding on the thread and screw it down to the forked end of the rod.

Special Notes

Before removing the brake shoes, have ready some means of retaining each operating piston in its cylinder—a length of wire or twine will do. Otherwise, owing to the slight residual pressure that is maintained in the braking system, the piston will tend to creep outwards, resulting in loss of fluid and entry of air into the system. Make a note of the way in which the pull-off springs are fitted in the shoes.

If oil or grease has leaked from the hub bearings, the oil seal in the hub must be renewed.

It is seldom advisable to clean oil-soaked linings with petrol or paraffin and it is also false economy to purchase cheap linings from a cut-price supplier, or to attempt to rivet new linings to the existing shoes, unless an efficient lining clamp is used. The safest plan is to fit factory-relined shoes.

If the brake drums are badly scored, have them reground or fit new drums.

It is always advisable to renew the pull-off springs when fitting replacement shoes. Weak springs can cause brake judder or squeal. Some old hands recommend that the ends of the new linings should be bevelled-off to prevent these troubles, but bevelling the leading edges of the linings is apt to cause or contribute to the faults, rather than cure them. The edges of the linings should be perfectly clean and square.

When the brakes have been reassembled, operate the handbrake lever at each backplate until the clicking of the adjuster ceases, indicating that the brakes are properly adjusted. *Make sure that the operating lever returns to the fully-off position at each stroke.*

Fitting New Friction Pads to Disc Brakes

It is not necessary to remove the disc brake calliper from the car or to separate the two halves of the unit, in order to renew the disc brake pads. *No attempt should be made to dismantle the calliper, in fact, unless proper equipment and the detailed instructions issued by the manufacturers are available.*

The friction pads in Girling brake callipers are retained by pins which are locked by spring clips. Lockheed friction pads are held in position by a crimped spring retainer which is held in place by long split-pins. Figs. 30 and 31 show the two arrangements.

To remove the pads:

1 Withdraw the pad-retaining pins or split-pins, and, on Lockheed brakes, the spring pad retainer.

2 Ease the pads and anti-squeal shims (when fitted) out of the calliper. It may be necessary to use a pair of thin-nosed pliers to extract the pads. Make sure that the replacement pads are of exactly the same type as those taken out.

3 Clean the exposed end of each piston thoroughly and make sure that

the recesses in the calliper which receive the friction pads are free from rust and grit. Sticking pistons or pads are a common cause of poor or uneven braking.

4 Release the bleed screw and lever each piston back into the calliper, being careful not to rotate it. Part of the rim of a Lockheed piston is cut back slightly and this relieved section must be positioned downwards and tilted slightly to the rear, as shown in Fig. 32. To avoid any risk of the fluid which is displaced by the movement of the pistons overflowing from the brake master cylinder, it is as well to ask an assistant to keep a watchful eye on the fluid level, ready, if necessary, to syphon-off any excess fluid from the reservoir.

5 Fit the pads into their recesses, making sure that they do not bind. If necessary, any high spots should be removed from the pads by careful filing.

6 Replace the retaining springs and pins in position. Preferably fit *new* split pins. Tighten the bleed screw.

7 Pump the brake pedal several times to adjust the brakes and then top-up the master cylinder reservoir to the correct level. It is not necessary to bleed the brakes after fitting new pads.

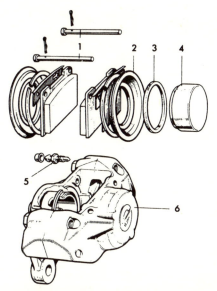

Fig. 30. Girling front disc-brake calliper

1, pad-retaining pins. 2, dust seal. 3, piston seal. 4, piston. 5, bleed screw. 6, calliper

36-4: Servicing the Hydraulic Components

The flexible brake hoses and the rubber pistons and seals in the hydraulic system should be renewed at 36,000 miles (60,000 km) or every three years. It should not be necessary to stress the serious consequences that may arise if a minor component if the hydraulic system should fail.

Repair kits containing complete sets of rubber parts for the various components are available, but assessment of the amount of wear or deterioration of the parts calls for experience and it is best to leave this sort of work to a dealer.

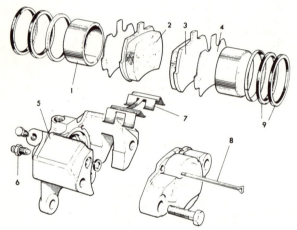

Fig. 31. Lockheed front disc-brake calliper

1, piston. 2, pad friction lining. 3, pad. 4, shim. 5, calliper. 6, bleed screw. 7, pad-retaining spring.
8, spring-retaining pin. 9, piston seals

In some cases faulty braking can be traced to a choked flexible hose. A new hose—or a set of new hoses—should be fitted if there is the slightest doubt about the condition of those in service, especially if they have been chafed on the outside.

A hose should never be subjected to any twisting strain. The correct method of installing it is first to attach the appropriate end to the wheel backplate or calliper and then to fit the shake-proof washer and tighten the union nut on the steel pipeline while holding the hose union securely with a second spanner.

Vacuum Servo. When a servo is provided it is mounted in the engine compartment. It requires no attention, except to renew the air filter after about 36,000 miles (60,000 km) in service—*see* below.

If the servo does not operate, first check that there is no leakage at the unions in the hose connecting it to the inlet manifold, and that the hose itself is not perished or collapsed. If all seems to be in order here, ask your dealer to vet the servo. If the trouble is more than a trivial fault and the servo has seen considerable service, it is fairly usual nowadays to fit a reconditioned unit under the service-exchange scheme operated by the manufacturers.

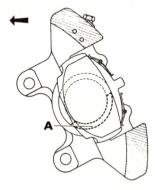

Fig. 32. The cut-out section of a Lockheed piston, A, should be downwards and slightly to the rear. The arrow indicates the front of the car

Should the servo fail for any reason, fluid can still flow through it to the brakes, but a considerably heavier pressure on the brake pedal will be required to obtain the same braking power.

36-5: Renewing the Servo Air Filter

The air filter surrounds the servo rod which is linked to the brake pedal. It can be reached from inside the driving compartment on right-hand drive models, or from the engine compartment on left-hand-drive vehicles, on which the servo is connected to the brake pedal by a relay lever and push-rod.

To renew the filter:

1 Pull back the corrugated rubber dust cover and the cup which retains the filter.
2 Prise out the filter and make a radial cut so that it can be detached from the rod.
3 Make a similar cut in the new filter, fit it around the rod and press it into the bore of the servo.
4 Press the retainer on to the end of the servo and refit the dust cover, making sure that it is located over all the lugs on the end-cover of the servo.

10 The steering, suspension, wheels and tyres

GOOD steering, first-class roadholding and satisfactory tyre life depend on a number of interrelated factors. The steering gear, suspension, shock absorbers and tyres all enter the picture to some extent. Maintenance of the correct steering "geometry," which can be upset by a minor kerb collision, to take one example, is particularly important. The castor, camber and swivel-pin angles of the front wheels are determined during the initial assembly of the suspension, and are not adjustable. Steering geometry checks and any necessary replacements must therefore be left to your dealer. They should preferably be carried out at 6,000-miles (10,000-km) intervals (especially if the rate of wear of the front tyres seems suspiciously high), and certainly during the 12,000-miles, 20,000-km, service.

The Steering Gear. The rack-and-pinion steering gear is mounted in rubber-insulated brackets attached to the front crossmember of the car. Either a Cam Gears or a Burman unit may be fitted. The complete assemblies are interchangeable, but the individual parts of the two gears are not.

Rotation of the steering wheel is transmitted by the steering column, through a flexible coupling, to the pinion of the steering unit, which moves the rack from side to side. Each end of the rack is coupled by a track-rod to the steering arm on the wheel hub.

The ball joints which couple the inner ends of the track rods to the steering rack are lubricated from the rack itself and are protected by corrugated rubber bellows. The outer joints are lubricated on assembly and are protected by gaiters. They do not need further lubrication during their normal life. When they develop wear, they must be renewed.

The rack bellows and the gaiters on the joints should, however, be inspected during routine servicing. Apart from allowing lubricant to escape, a damaged gaiter or bellows will also allow water and grit to enter the joint or the rack, quickly rendering it unserviceable.

A quarter of a pint of SAE 90 hypoid oil is poured into the rack housing when it is assembled and the rack should not require further lubrication unless a gaiter has been damaged or a clip has slackened-off, allowing oil to escape. The steering gear should on no account be completely filled with oil, as this will result in a pressure build-up which could burst the gaiters or blow them off the ends of the rack.

Even when the gear contains the correct amount of oil, never swing the roadwheels quickly from lock to lock while the car is jacked-up, as this may generate sufficient hydraulic pressure to damage or to dislodge the gaiters.

Two adjustments are provided to take up wear in the steering gear. To adjust the rack damper or the pinion bearing pre-load, the thickness of a shim-pack beneath a cover plate must be varied. It is necessary to remove the gear from the car to do this and the work should normally be left to your dealer, as special tools must be used to measure the pinion turning torque and the tightness of the track-rod ball joints.

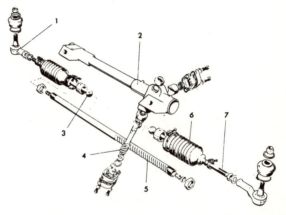

Fig. 33. A typical steering assembly, in this case the Burman design

1, outer ball joint. 2, rack housing. 3, inner tracked-rod joint. 4, pinion. 5, rack. 6, protective gaiter. 7, adjustable end of track-rod

The alignment of the front wheels is set by adjusting the lengths of the track rods and again this should be done only when an accurate wheel-alignment gauge is available. Makeshift methods of checking the toe-in usually lead to heavy tyre wear.

Wheel Balancing. Before leaving the subject of the steering, the importance of wheel and tyre balance must be emphasized. Wheel-wobble and quite severe vibration at about 60–80 m.p.h. (100–130 k.p.h.), and sometimes at lower speeds, can be caused by unbalanced wheels and tyres. It is advisable to have the balance checked by a properly equipped garage every 3,000 miles (5,000 km), preferably with the aid of a dynamic balancer which allows the degree of unbalance to be checked electronically when the wheel is spun without removing it from the front hub.

The rear wheels should be balanced at the same time. They can not only cause vibration, but may also cause a rear-end steering effect if they are badly out of balance.

The Front Suspension. The independent front suspension incorporates a coil spring on each side of the car, fitted between upper and lower suspension arms which are pivoted to the front cross-member at their inner ends, and to the stub-axle carrier—termed the steering knuckle—at the outer ends. Additional location for each lower arm is provided by an adjustable control rod.

A telescopic hydraulic shock absorber is fitted inside each coil spring, attached at its upper end to the cross-member and at its lower end to the lower suspension arm.

The steering knuckle is attached to the suspension arms by upper and lower ball-joints, each of which is provided with a lubrication nipple.

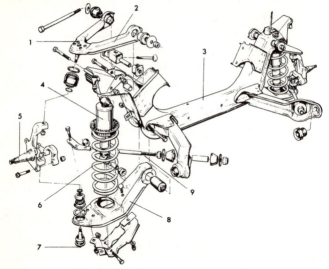

Fig. 34. The front suspension assembly

1, upper ball joint lubricator. 2, upper suspension arm. 3, axle cross-member. 4, shock absorber. 5, steering knuckle. 6, suspension spring. 7, lower ball joint. 8, lower suspension arm, 9, control rod

The front suspension needs no routine maintenance, apart from lubricating the upper and lower ball-joints on each side at 6,000-miles intervals checking the ball-joints and rubber bushes for wear, making sure that the various attachment nuts and bolts are kept tight, and servicing the wheel hub bearings, as described later.

6-15: Checking the Front Suspension Joints for Wear

Remember when checking the suspension ball-joints, that the seatings for the balls are loaded by neoprene rubber rings which normally eliminate any vertical clearance in the joint. To check the joints:

1 Raise the front wheels and support the car under the lower suspension arms.
2 Rock the wheels vertically and horizontally, while holding the upper and lower joints in turn. If any perceptible slackness can be felt in the joint, replacements must be fitted. This is normally a job for your Vauxhall dealer.

12-6: Servicing the Front-wheel Bearings

During the 12,000-mile (20,000-km) service the front-wheel hub bearings should be removed for inspection and repacked with grease. On reassembly they must be adjusted so that they are neither too tight nor too loose. The novice would be well-advised to leave this work to a Vauxhall dealer, especially when disc brakes are fitted, since it is then necessary to disconnect the front brake pipes and remove the brake callipers.

If you propose to do the work yourself and your car has disc front brakes, buy a set of new calliper attachment bolts. Each bolt has a nylon insert at the outer end of the thread which provides a self-locking action. Once a bolt has been fitted and removed, however, the self-locking effect can no longer be relied on—hence the need for fitting new bolts.

The sequence in servicing the bearings is as follows:

1 Remove the wheel and prise off the hub dust cap, which is a push-fit in the hub.
2 When disc front brakes are fitted, remove the brake calliper, after first taking out the brake pads (*see* page 78) and unscrewing the brake pipe union on the bracket on the steering knuckle. Plug both the end of the pipe and the union to prevent the entry of dirt or grit.
3 Withdraw the split-pin, remove the nut retainer, unscrew the hub-retaining nut and pull off the hub.
4 Wash all parts in paraffin. Look for any broken rollers, scored or pitted tracks or signs of "blueing" caused by overheating. Any of these faults will, of course, call for new bearings.
5 Check the condition of the oil seal. Drum-brake models have a felt sealing ring, disc-brake models a spring-loaded lip-type seal, which must be installed with the lip and the spring facing *into* the hub. Make sure that the seat for the seal on the stub axle is perfectly clean. If any trace of corrosion is not polished off, the effective life of the seal will be reduced. Lip-type oil seals should be lubricated during assembly with Rocol anti-scuffing paste, which can be obtained from a Vauxhall dealer.

6 Pack the bearings and the hub half-full with clean grease and reassemble. *Do not* fill the hub completely. Space must be left for expansion as the hub warms up during normal running.

7 Adjust the bearings. Tighten the hub-retaining nut with a tubular spanner until a slight drag is felt when the hub is rotated. Slacken back the nut, remove the tommy-bar and retighten the nut by using hand pressure only to turn the spanner.

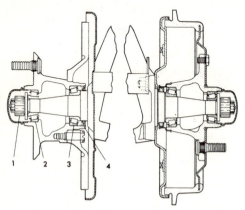

Fig. 35. Front hub assemblies: *left*, as used with a disc-brake and *right*, with a drum-brake assembly

1, hub-nut retainer. 2, outer bearing. 3, inner bearing. 4, grease seal

8 Refit the nut retainer, trying it in different positions until one of the slots lines-up with the split-pin hole in the end of the stub axle. Fit a new split pin, bend over the ends and refit the dust cap.

9 Where necessary, refit the brake calliper, reconnect the brake pipe and bleed the brakes as described in Chapter 9.

Special Notes

If the wheel bearings are too tightly adjusted the hub will overheat. If there is too much play, the brake-pad piston will be knocked back into the calliper, giving excessive pedal travel.

Plastic golf-ball tees can be used to plug the open ends of the brake pipes to prevent loss of fluid and to exclude dirt and grit.

The Rear Suspension. The rear axle is carried on a pair of lower arms, pivoted at their forward ends and supported by coil springs. A pair of short upper arms, connected transversely between the underframe and the axle on each side of the differential housing, control lateral movement of the axle. Telescopic hydraulic shock absorbers are fitted between the underframe and brackets at the outer ends of the axle. The upper shock-absorber mountings can be reached from inside the luggage compartment after removing rubber plugs which seal the access holes on each side of the raised section at the front of the compartment.

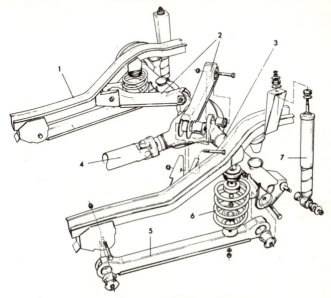

Fig. 36. The rear suspension components

1, underbody frame member. 2, diagonally-mounted upper arm. 3, rear axle. 4, propellor shaft. 5, lower suspension arm. 6, suspension spring. 7, shock absorber

The Shock Absorbers. The front and rear shock absorbers do not, of course, have an unlimited life. When they become worn they will affect the steering, roadholding and the comfort of the ride. After about 30,000 miles (48,000 km) it is as well to have the shock absorbers checked by a dealer, preferably using a special test rig which enables their effectiveness to be accurately measured and recorded. Weak shock absorbers should be renewed without delay. They could cause a fatal accident.

The Tyres. Apart from regular pressure checks, most authorities agree that a longer life can be obtained from a set of ordinary cross-ply tyres by changing them round at 3,000-mile (5,000-km) intervals, to equalize the wear on the individual treads. If the wheels are not changed around, there is the risk, in these day of extended service periods, that damage to the inside walls of a tyre may pass unnoticed. Uneven wear caused by misalignment of the wheels can also escape detection.

When radial-ply tyres are fitted, however (and radials greatly improve the already good steering and roadholding), it is an advantage to interchange the tyres from side to side at 3,000-mile (5,000-km) intervals, but they should not be exchanged from front to rear. The tyres on the front wheels develop a different form of tread wear from those at the rear. If they are changed around when the characteristic wear pattern has become established, roadholding and steering will suffer.

Radial-ply tyres should never be fitted to the front wheels only, with cross-ply tyres at the rear. *There are no exceptions to this rule and to ignore it can be dangerous.* As a temporary measure, radials can be fitted to the *rear* wheels only, but the only really satisfactory course is to change the complete set.

When rapid tread wear occurs on the front tyres, have the steering geometry and the alignment of the front wheels checked as recommended earlier. An error of $\frac{1}{2}$ in. in alignment will have the same effect as dragging a spinning tyre sideways for nearly 90 feet in every mile on the road!

Also remember that speed costs money: tyres wear twice as quickly at 65 m.p.h. as at 35 m.p.h. and fast cornering, rapid acceleration and heavy braking must all be paid for in terms of tread rubber left on the road. Another sobering thought—a 10 per cent reduction in tyre pressure below the recommended figure will result in an average loss of 13 per cent in tread mileage.

Puncture Repairs. A tubeless tyre can usually be repaired by "plugging" but this should be regarded strictly as a temporary repair. *The tyre should be removed and a proper vulcanized repair carried out as soon as possible.* Until this can be done, speeds should be kept down to about 50 m.p.h.

There is another important point which is often overlooked: when a new tubeless tyre is fitted, a new snap-in tyre valve should be fitted at the same time. The valve will last the life of a tyre, but after that there is always the risk or leakage between the base of the valve and the wheel rim.

Using a Jack. The jack engages with two points on each side of the car. Whenever possible, avoid jacking when the car is on a slope: if this is unavoidable, the handbrake should be applied really firmly and should be reinforced, if possible, by placing a chock behind one of the wheels that is not being jacked-up. If the wheel to be removed is on the side nearest the kerb, make sure that there will be sufficient space to slide the wheel off its studs when the car is lifted.

And finally—never be tempted to work beneath the car when it is supported only by the jack. Always place really secure blocks beneath the axles or the frame. Better still, use properly designed wheel ramps or axle-stands.

11 The electrical equipment

In this chapter, we shall be dealing mostly with routine maintenance of the electrical equipment, but some notes will be included on simple fault-tracing and first-aid measures.

The main components of the system are the alternator or generator, with its associated battery-charging circuit, the battery itself, the starter motor, the lighting equipment and the electrically-operated accessories, such as the horns, direction indicators and windscreen wipers.

Strictly speaking, the ignition system should be included in the electrical equipment, but correct maintenance of the ignition system and accurate setting of the ignition timing is so important that Chapter 6 has been devoted to these subjects.

The Battery Charging Circuit. The electrical generator is driven by a belt from the engine crankshaft pulley. It charges the battery and also supplies current to operate the ignition system and the electrical accessories when the engine is running.

An alternator is fitted to all models, instead of a dynamo. This has the advantage that a useful amount of current is generated even at a fast idling speed.

The charging rate of the generator is automatically regulated to suit the state of charge of the battery, the prevailing atmospheric temperature, and the current that is being drawn by the various circuits at any given moment.

The regulator provides a large charging current (up to the maximum output of the generator) when the battery is discharged, the rate being highest in cold weather. As the battery voltage rises, the charging rate is reduced, tapering off to a "trickle" charge that keeps a fully-charged battery in good condition.

The 12-volt battery provides the reserve of current that is needed to start the engine, and to operate the lights and any accessories that may be in use when the engine is not running, or when it is idling. At idling speeds, the alternator does not produce any useful current, and a red warning light on the instrument panel glows whenever this occurs.

Although this lamp is usually termed the ignition warning light (because one of its functions is to remind you not to leave the ignition on when the engine is not running) it has the equally important function of warning that the alternator is not charging. It should therefore be regarded as an *ignition and no-charge* warning light.

If the light does not go out, or glows faintly whenever the engine is speeded-up above idling speed, the battery is not receiving a charge and will quickly become discharged if the trouble is not put right without delay. First check that the fan belt is intact and correctly tensioned; then have the generator and regulator checked by an electrical specialist, or make the tests described later in this chapter.

ROUTINE MAINTENANCE

No special electrical knowledge, or expensive test instruments, are needed for normal maintenance of the electrical equipment, nor should simple fault-tracing and first-aid measures present any problems. If any serious troubles crop-up, it is best to take advantage of the service-exchange scheme operated by your dealer, under which a faulty component is replaced by a reconditioned, guaranteed unit at a fixed charge.

When removing and replacing the battery, or when working on the system, remember that the *negative* battery terminal is earthed. As there will be both positive-earth and negative-earth systems in use on British cars for some years to come, special care must also be taken when ordering and installing replacement equipment and accessories such as a transistor-operated car radio, which will be seriously damaged if it is connected so that its polarity is reversed.

W-4: Topping-up the Battery Cells

The liquid in the cells (the electrolyte) tends to evaporate rather quickly, especially in hot weather.

1 Check the levels at weekly intervals.
2 Don't allow the electrolyte to fall below the tops of the separators between the plates, or the perforated separator guard, as the case may be.

Special Notes

Distilled or "purified" water is obtainable quite cheaply from chemists. Tapwater and rainwater may contain impurities that will shorten the life of the battery. In an emergency, water from the drip-tray of a refrigerator which has been defrosted can be used, but *not* the water obtained by melting ice cubes.

Never use a naked flame when inspecting the fluid level. An explosive mixture of hydrogen and oxygen is produced when the electrolyte begins to bubble, as the battery becomes fully charged.

Add water just before the cells are to be charged, to allow the acid and water to mix thoroughly, and to avoid any risk of the water freezing, expanding and damaging the plates and battery case in cold weather.

The need for frequent topping-up usually suggests too high a generator charging rate. If one cell regularly requires more water than the others, it is probably leaking. Unless the battery is nearly new, or still under guarantee, repairs to individual cells are not usually worthwhile.

It should not be necessary to add *acid* to the cells unless some of the electrolyte has been split, in which case it would be wise to have a word with your dealer.

Finally, remember that the electrolyte is a very corrosive solution of sulphuric acid in water. If any is spilled, wipe it away immediately with a clean wet cloth and then dry the part thoroughly. Household ammonia will neutralize the acid.

6-18: Battery Maintenance

The tops of the cells must be kept clean and dry, to prevent corrosion of the terminals and leakage of current.

To clean the terminals and terminal posts:

1 Take off the connectors.
2 Scrape any corrosion off the terminals.
3 Replace the connectors and tighten the retaining screws. Smear the terminals and posts with petroleum jelly to protect them against corrosion.

Special Notes

Don't overlook the connections at the earthed end of the battery earthing strap, at the starter motor and at the solenoid switch, mounted on the right-hand side of the engine compartment bulkhead. These connections must be clean and secure.

The battery-retaining clamp should be just sufficiently tight to prevent movement of the battery on its mounting. Overtightening it may crack or distort the battery case.

Servicing an Alternator. An alternator requires no routine maintenance, except for keeping the terminals clean and the end-plate free from deposits of dust and grease. There are, however, several practical points to be remembered when dealing with an alternator which may be overlooked by an owner who has previously dealt only with dynamos.

If the battery has been removed, when refitting it first connect the negative battery terminal to the earth strap and then fit the positive terminal connector. *Never disconnect the battery when the engine is running*.

Care must be taken not to earth the "live" connector in the moulded socket if it is removed from the alternator. Never run the engine with the main output cable from the alternator disconnected.

If a charger is to be used to charge-up a flat battery, first isolate the alternator by disconnecting both battery terminals.

An electrician who is not familiar with an alternator should be warned not to use an ohmmeter of the type that incorporates a hand-driven generator (usually known as a "megger") to check the rectifier diodes or the transistors in the circuit.

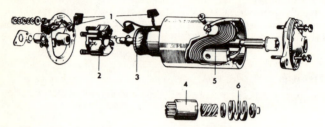

Fig. 37. Inertia-engaged starter motor used on later push-rod engines

1, brushes. 2, brush-holder. 3, face-type commutator. 4, pinion. 5, field coils. 6, pinion-drive spring

If the charging circuit gives trouble, or the alternator requires routine servicing, the work should always be done by a fully-qualified auto-electrician.

The Starter Motor. The starter motor is probably the most important of the auxiliaries that draw current from the battery. Unlike the generator, it is in action only intermittently and usually has a long, trouble-free life. Because it requires no periodic lubrication it is, in fact, often overlooked by the average owner.

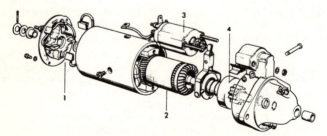

Fig. 38. This type of solenoid-engaged starter motor is used on many overhead-camshaft models

1, brush holder and brushes. 2, armature. 3, solenoid. 4, pinion assembly

36-2: Starter Motor Servicing

The starter should be serviced at reasonable intervals—say, every 36,000 miles (60,000 km)—when it should be removed from the car and dismantled by an expert, so that the commutator, brushes and the pinion-drive components can be inspected and cleaned.

The Headlamps. The headlamps are fitted either with sealed-beam light units or with separate reflectors and lamp bulbs. Sealed-beam units form, in effect, large bulbs, each with either one or two filaments, an integral reflector and a front lens. Consequently, when a filament burns-out, it is necessary to renew the complete unit. On some models, however, conventional reflector and front lens assemblies are fitted, and in this case the separate bulbs can be renewed.

It is particularly important that the headlamp beams should be correctly aligned. Hit-and-miss methods of adjustment in the home garage are likely to result in settings that dazzle oncoming traffic or do not give the most effective illumination.

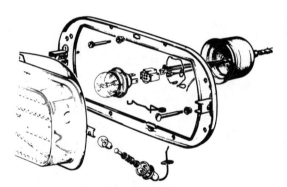

Fig. 39. Typical rectangular headlamp assembly incorporating headlamp and sidelamp bulbs

Most garages today, however, have optical beam-setting equipment which enables the lamps to be precisely adjusted. The headlamp settings should be checked with the aid of such equipment twice a year if a lot of night driving is done, or at least once every autumn.

Each unit has two beam-adjusting screws. One screw raises or lowers the beam and the other swings it from side to side. The screws extend into the engine compartment. It is preferable to use the special Vauxhall tool to rotate them if you intend to align the lamps yourself, although this is not essential.

Removing and Replacing Headlamp Bulbs or Light Units

When separate headlamp bulbs are fitted, these can be removed and replaced from inside the engine compartment.

1 Pull off the rubber dust cover and disconnect the wiring connector.
2 Ease back the spring clips and pull the bulb out of its holder.
3 When fitting a bulb notice that the flange is located by a projection which engages with a slot in the reflector body.

With four-lamp systems either sealed-beam units or Unified European pattern reflectors, fitted with separate bulbs, are used. To renew a light unit or a bulb:

1 Remove the radiator grille insert.
2 Slacken the three screws in the rim which retains the light unit or reflector and turn the rim anti-clockwise to free it.
3 Withdraw the light unit or reflector, unplug the connector and remove the bulb, when this is a separate fitting.

Special Notes

Removing or refitting a light or reflector unit does not disturb the aiming of the headlamps.

Removing and Replacing Side-lamp Bulbs

The sidelight bulbs are incorporated in the rectangular type of headlamp and the holder can simply be pulled out of its mounting. When circular headlamps are fitted, the sidelights are incorporated in the indicator lamps, each of which then has two single-filament bulbs.

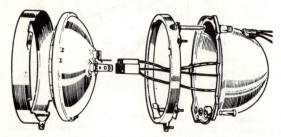

Fig. 40. Headlamp assembly using a one-piece light unit, instead of a separate reflector and bulb

Removing and Replacing Stop, Tail and Rear-indicator Lights

1 *Saloon models*. Remove the protective covers from inside the boot and pull out the bulb holders, which are a snap fit in the lamp body.

2 *Estate cars.* The protective covers are retained by three screws, along the upper edge of each cover.

3 *Number-plate lights.* These are mounted on brackets attached to the rear bumper. To change a bulb, remove the screw that secures the lamp rim, lift the rim away and pull the lens out of its rubber seating.

Removing and Replacing Instrument Panel Bulbs. The instrument illumination and warning lamp bulbs can be changed as follows:

Seven-dial instrument panels and panels incorporating strip-type speedometers. The bulb holders at the outer end of the instrument assembly can be pulled out of their seatings by reaching up behind the panel. The holders at the inner end of the instrument assembly can be reached when the "filler panel" next to the steering wheel, which carries the windscreen washer and cigarette lighter, has been removed by taking out four screws.

The bulbs in strip-type speedometer panels are the wedge-base capless type, in holders which are a push fit in the panel. When replacing these, hold them with the contacts horizontal and make sure that they click into place. On seven-dial panels, the bulbs in the warning display have bayonet-type holders which must be pressed in and turned anti-clockwise to remove them.

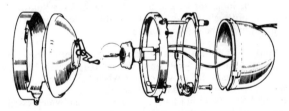

Fig. 41. Another type of reflector-and-bulb headlamp assembly

Two-dial instrument panels (with speedometer, fuel and temperature gauges and warning lamps). The bulbs in the warning lamp display at the side panel, and the speedometer illumination bulb, can be removed by reaching up above the parcel shelf on the driver's side. To remove the remaining bulbs, the instrument assembly must be detached and moved forward, after reaching up behind the panel to unscrew the speedometer cable retaining sleeve and taking out the four screws that retain the panel The bulbs are three-watt wedge-base capless type, in bayonet-type holders which must be pressed in and turned anti-clockwise to remove them.

Removing and Replacing Lamp in Console. When a console is fitted, it may be a one-piece moulding, in which case it is necessary to remove the whole assembly to change the bulbs. In other cases a detachable insert gives access to the bulbs.

The Windscreen Wiper. The electrically-operated wiper normally requires no attention, other than renewal of the wiper blades at least once a year. Always use a screen-wash solvent in the washer water. Use an anti-freeze type in winter. Radiator anti-freeze is unsuitable.

If the blades do not sweep through satisfactory arcs, or fail to park neatly when the wiper is switched off (they are self-parking), the arms may have been incorrectly fitted to the driving spindles. They can be withdrawn by depressing the spring catch that clamps the arm to the splined section of the spindle or, if a screw is fitted, by slackening this and tapping it inwards to release the tapered wedge. Refit the arm in the desired position and push it fully home.

Wet the screen before checking the sweep and the parking of the blades. A test on a dry screen will give misleading results, owing to excessive friction between the blades and the glass.

Flashing Indicators. The flashing-indicator lamps are fed with current from a sealed control unit, secured by a spring clip in the lower half of the steering-column cowl. If either a front or a rear indicator bulb should fail, the remaining indicators will continue to flash, but at a faster rate than normal.

Failure or erratic action of the indicators may also be caused by dirty contacts in the indicator switch, in the wiring, or by a "blown" fuse. If the fuse is in order, the flasher unit is probably faulty. It is not repairable. To renew it, lower the steering-column cowl.

The Brake-light Switch. This switch is screwed into a bracket on the pedal assembly in the driving compartment. It is operated by the brake pedal, the contacts in the switch closing when the pressure on the switch plunger is released as the pedal is pressed down.

If the brake lights do not light-up when the pedal is depressed, switch on the ignition, disconnect the leads from the switch terminals and connect them together. If the brake lights then operate, the switch is faulty, or the connections to it were dirty or corroded. If the lights still fail to operate, the fault must lie in the fuse (*see* page 97) or in the wiring or connections in the circuit.

To renew the switch:

1 Pull off the wiring connectors.
2 Depress the brake pedal and remove the pedal-stop rubber from the switch plunger.
3 Unscrew the hexagonal retaining-nut and withdraw the switch from the bracket.
4 Fit the new switch and adjust the two nuts so that when the brake pedal is right back, the switch contacts just break (check that the light goes out with the ignition switched on). If the switch is set so that the plunger is fully depressed, the brake pedal may have too little free travel,

causing the brakes to bind, and there is also a risk that the switch may be damaged.

Fuses and Protection against Short-circuits. The electrical system is protected against overloading or short-circuits in three ways: by four fuses, housed in a plug-in connector on the engine bulkhead, by a thermal circuit breaker which protects the lighting circuits, and by a fusible link— a sort of super-fuse which is connected into the main battery feed, and which protects the entire electrical circuit with the exception of the starter.

Failure of a particular fuse is indicated when the circuit protected by it becomes "dead." If a new fuse burns out immediately, find the cause and rectify the fault before fitting a new fuse having the same rating, which is shown on a coloured slip of paper inside the fuse. Always fit a fuse of the correct rating and *never be tempted to bridge the fuse-holder clips with ordinary wire*, as this can lead to a fire in the wiring, or a burnt-out component.

Fuses. The bulkhead connector contains four 35-amp fuses and two spares. Number 4 fuse is fed from the thermal interruptor and lighting switch. The circuits protected are:

Fuse No. 1   .   .   Horn, interior lamp, headlamp flasher, electric clock, hazard-warning unit.

Fuse No. 2   .   .   Stop lamps, indicator lamps and warning lamps, oil and ignition/alternator warning lamps, fuel and temperature gauges, heater motor, reversing lamps, voltage stabilizer, tachometer, heated rear window.

Fuse No. 3   .   .   Windscreen wipers, radio, cigarette lighter, electric windscreen washer.

Fuse No. 4   .   .   Console and instrument panel lamps, rear lamps, number-plate lamps, luggage compartment lamps, cigarette lighter bulb, fog lamps.

Thermal Interruptor. This protects the headlights, sidelights and the fog lights, if fitted. If the current in a circuit becomes excessive, the thermal interruptor will rapidly make-and-break the circuit. This will reduce the current sufficiently to prevent damage, but will usually provide sufficient illumination from the lights to enable the car to be driven to a service station. Since fuse No. 4 is fed through the interruptor, a lighting defect which brings the interruptor into action would also cause apparent defects in the operation of the other lights which are fed from this fuse.

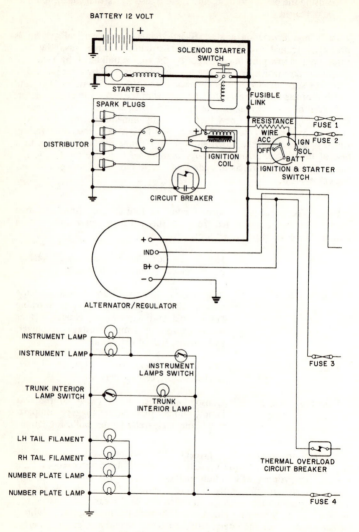

Fig. 42. Theoretical wiring diagram

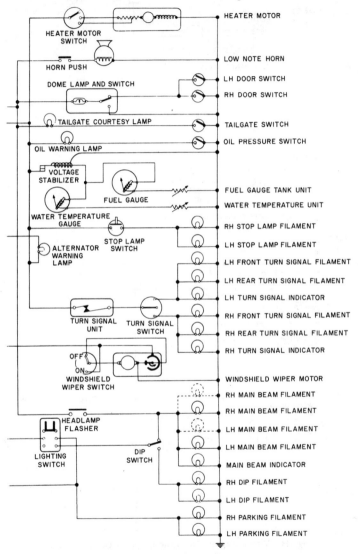

Fig. 42 (continued).

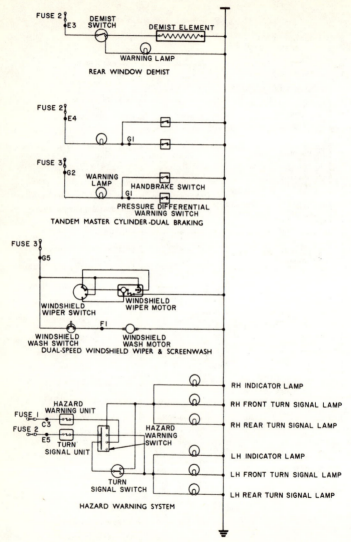

Fig. 43. Wiring diagram for optional electrical equipment

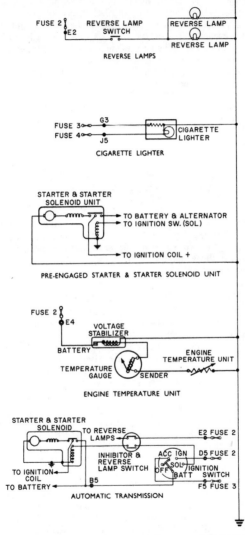

Fig. 44. Wiring diagram for automatic transmission models

Fusible Link. The fusible link is plugged on to a connector on the terminal block which is mounted on the battery support tray. On a car which has an inertia-engaged starter, the other end of the link is connected to the main feed terminal on the starter solenoid switch, attached to the end of the battery tray. When a pre-engaged starter is fitted the end of the link is plugged into an insulated terminal, connected into the heavy battery-to-starter cable, attached to the end of the battery tray and protected by a cover. The special insulation used on the link will not burn or disintegrate if the link should fuse.

If total failure of the electrical system, with the exception of the starter, is experienced, obviously the first points to check are that the connections at each end of the link are clean and secure and that the link itself has not fused.

SIMPLE FAULT-TRACING

A thorough diagnosis of an ailing electrical system calls for the use of proper fault-tracing equipment, or at the least, an accurate moving-coil voltmeter. Ideally, a Smiths Automotive Electrical Instrument Tester, SR/D366 or 380 should be used to check the fuel and temperature gauges, so this sort of work is outside the scope of the average owner.

There are, however, some simple tests that can be made when it is suspected that the generator is not giving its full charge, or when the starter motor does not turn the engine.

5-18: Testing the Generator and Charging System

The following tests, for which only a voltmeter is required, are sufficient to show whether or not all is well with the alternator and charging system. A moving-coil type of meter is to be preferred, but any good-quality instrument can be used, as the checks depend on comparative readings, rather than on exact voltages. They are based on the fact that the battery voltage varies according to the state of charge, and is always higher when the cells are receiving a charge from the alternator.

To make the test:

1 Clip the voltmeter leads to the battery terminals, making sure that the surface of the metal has been pierced. If the battery is sound and well charged, a reading of 12–12·5 volts should be obtained.
2 Switch on all the lights. The reading should now fall to approximately 11–11·5 volts.
3 Start the engine and speed it up to the equivalent of about 20 m.p.h. in top gear, but do not race it. The reading should now be about 13·5 volts, and the voltmeter needle should be steady. If it flickers, there may be a bad contact in the wiring, the alternator windings may be dirty, the brushes may be worn or sticking, or the regulator may be faulty.

Special Notes

If voltage readings roughly equal to those quoted are obtained, it can be assumed that the battery and charging system are sound. If the voltage across the battery does not rise by 1 volt when the engine is speeded-up above idling speed, there is a fault somewhere in the charging system, probably one of those just mentioned. If the increase exceeds about 1·5 volts, either the regulator is incorrectly adjusted or the battery is faulty. Do not try to adjust the regulator. Leave this sort of work to a qualified auto-electrician.

Testing a Faulty Starter Motor

1 Switch on the lights and press the starter switch. If the solenoid switch clicks and the lights go dim, but the starter does not operate, either the battery is discharged or current is flowing through the windings of the starter but for some reason the armature is not rotating. Probably the starter pinion is jammed in mesh with the flywheel starter ring. To free it, *see Special Notes*, below.

2 If the lamps remain bright, the starter switch may be faulty, but first check for loose or corroded connections on the ignition switch or on the electro-magnetic solenoid starter switch itself, which is mounted on the engine bulkhead.

Special Notes

To free a jammed starter pinion, switch off the ignition, engage *top gear* and rock the car *forwards*. Do not rock the car backwards and forwards, as this may jam the pinion more firmly in mesh with the flywheel ring-gear teeth.

12 When things go wrong

THE risk of an unexpected breakdown must obviously be greatly reduced by regular servicing. The work described in previous chapters can therefore be described as *preventive* maintenance in the best sense of the word; it aims at detecting or forestalling trouble before it becomes serious. Most faults, in fact, can be traced back to neglect at some stage. Dirt, lack of lubrication or incorrect adjustment are the most frequent culprits.

In the charts in this chapter it has been possible to deal only with the simpler checks that can be made in the garage or by the roadside. It is assumed that special test equipment will not be available, and that expert help will be called in if the trouble does not respond to first-aid measures.

The secret of diagnosing a fault quickly is to follow a systematic process of elimination. Haphazard tests seldom pay dividends—although there are, of course, occasions on which the possibility of a particular fault can be assumed with a fair amount of certainty. Take the case of a normally well-behaved engine that refuses to fire from cold after the car has been parked in the open during a spell of damp, misty weather. Condensation on the high-tension leads, ignition coil, distributor, and sparking-plug insulators is almost a certainty, and a spray with one of the water-repelling Aerosol fluids, or a wipe with a dry cloth with usually be all that is needed to restore normal starting.

Similarly, if an engine runs well, but is a brute to start from cold, suspect too weak a starting mixture. Make sure that the mixture control is operating properly and that the petrol pump is delivering plenty of fuel. If the engine is reluctant to start when hot, on the other hand, check for an over-rich mixture. In either case, if the carburation seems to be satisfactory, the ignition system should be carefully checked-over, following the step-by-step charts in this chapter.

Once a year, or before starting a holiday tour, there is a great deal to be said for taking the car to a garage which has electronic test-tune equipment, with which every aspect of the ignition system, carburation and mechanical efficiency can be quickly checked and any faults or maladjustments pinpointed quickly and accurately.

STARTING TROUBLES

Starter Motor Faults

Starter Motor Does Not Turn Engine

Probable Fault
Battery discharged or worn-out.
Battery connections or earthing strap loose or corroded.
Faulty starter switch.
Dirty starter drive.
Drive spring broken.
Faulty starter motor.
Engine water pump frozen.

Starter Operates but Pinion Will Not Engage with Flywheel Ring Gear

Dirt or excessive wear on pinion drive, preventing the control nut running along the screwed sleeve. Removal of the starter, cleaning the drive and renewal of any worn parts will usually cure the trouble. Low battery voltage is also a possible cause.
When a pre-engaged starter is fitted, check the solenoid-operated engagement mechanism.

Turns Engine Slowly

Probable Fault
Battery partly discharged or nearing end of life.
Battery connections or earthing strap loose or corroded.
Too heavy a grade of engine oil in use.
Faulty starter motor.

Dirt or grit on pinion sleeve.
Badly worn or damaged teeth on pinion or on flywheel ring gear.

Pinion Will Not Disengage

If the pinion is jammed in mesh with the flywheel ring gear, a click will be heard from the starter solenoid switch when the key switch is turned. To free the pinion, see page 103

Excessively Noisy Starter

Loose starter-mounting bolts or worn or damaged pinion or flywheel ring gear.

STARTING TROUBLES (contd.)

Engine Will Not Fire

Carry out the following checks in sequence (see text)

Ignition System *Probable Fault*	Fuel System Check	Fuel System *Probable Fault*
	Check that petrol reaches carburettor when engine is rotated by starter, by disconnecting pipe at carburettor. *Do not:* allow petrol to drip on to hot exhaust pipe; allow sparks to occur; while making test.	

Battery Check
Switch on lights and check brightness when starter is operated.

Lamps do not light, or are weak—

Battery discharged (see also page 111).
Battery connections or earthing strap loose or corroded.

Lights dim only slightly—

Faulty ignition switch.
Loose connection or broken wire between switch and ignition coil or distributor.

Fuel System Check

No petrol reaching carburettor—

Petrol tank empty.
Choked petrol filter.
Air leak in pipeline.
Faulty petrol pump.
Air vent to tank clogged.
Blockage in pipeline.

Sparking plug Check
Remove a plug, reconnect the lead and lay the plug on the cylinder block. Watch for sparks while the engine is rotated.

No spark at plug gap—

Condensed moisture on distributor cap or plug leads or insulators.
Oil or condensed fuel or water on plug points or interval insulator.

Sparking-plug internal or external insulator dirty or cracked.
Ignition system trouble (see below).

Petrol reaching carburettor—

Mixture too rich or too weak.
Water in petrol.
Bad air-leak in induction manifold or at carburettor flange.

Distributor Check
Remove sparking plug lead from plug, hold bare end of connector ¼ in. from unpainted metal of engine. Rotate engine with ignition switched on.

No spark from sparking plug lead—

Contact-breaker points dirty or pitted, or not opening and closing.
Cracked rotor.
Poor connection in low-tension circuit.
Faulty distributor cap.
Faulty condenser or connections.
Spring contact on rotor faulty.
High-tension coil lead loose or broken.

OTHER POSSIBLE CAUSES OF DIFFICULT STARTING
Broken distributor drive.
Timing-chain broken or has jumped sprocket teeth.
Exhaust tailpipe blocked.

Spark from lead—

Coil burnt out.
Trouble must lie in sparking plugs.

MISCELLANEOUS ENGINE TROUBLES

SYMPTOM	Ignition	Fuel System	Other Faults
Misfiring	Incorrect gap at sparking-plug points. Dirty or cracked sparking-plug insulators. Wrong type of sparking plugs. Damp or oily deposits on high-tension leads, sparking plug, distributor or coil insulation. High-tension or low-tension leads loose or short-circuiting. Faulty ignition interference suppressors (if fitted) or plug leads. Condensation on plug points. Low-tension connection loose. Broken wire in distributor between capacitor and contact-breaker points. Faulty ignition-switch contact. Contact-breaker rocker arm sticking. Dirty contact-breaker points.	Water in carburettor. Petrol pipe partly blocked. Fuel pump pressure low. Fuel pump filter choked. Carburettor needle valve faulty or dirty. Jet blocked. Piston sticking.	Incorrect valve-clearance. Valves sticking. Valve seatings burnt. Valve spring broken. Leaking cylinder-head gasket.
Engine Fires but Will Not Continue to Run		Carburettor needle valve sticking. Fuel pump faulty. Petrol pipe partly blocked. Jet blocked. Water in petrol.	Exhaust tailpipe obstructed. Incorrect ignition or valve timing.
Engine Runs on Wide Throttle Opening Only		Slow-running mixture strength and/or idling speed incorrect. Jet blocked. Air leak at carburettor or inlet manifold flange.	Valves sticking. Valve seatings burnt. Valve spring broken.
Engine Does Not Give Full Power	Ignition timing retarded. Ignition timing over-advanced. Ignition faults (see under *Misfiring*).	Petrol supply troubles (see above). Throttle not opening fully. Jet blocked. Piston sticking. Carburettor throttles need synchronizing (twin carburetors only).	Incorrect valve clearances. Valve seatings burnt. Partial engine seizure—(see *Overheating*). Leaking cylinder-head gasket. Low compression due to worn piston rings and cylinders.

PROBABLE CAUSE

MISCELLANEOUS ENGINE TROUBLES (contd.)

SYMPTOM	PROBABLE CAUSE		
	Ignition	*Fuel System*	*Other Faults*
Overheating	Ignition timing incorrect—too far advanced or retarded.	Weak mixture (see under *Mis-firing*).	Filler cap not retaining pressure in cooling system.
	Wrong type of sparking plug, over-heating and causing pre-ignition.		Too little water in radiator.
			Fan belt slipping or broken.
			Choked radiator (water and air passages).
			Lime and rust deposits in cooling system.
			Perished or collapsed water hoses.
			Faulty thermostat.
			Leaking cylinder-head gasket.
			Too little oil in engine.
			Tight engine after overhaul.
Knocking or Pinking	Ignition timing too far advanced.	Wrong grade of fuel in use—use premium grade, if this does not cure trouble, check for faults listed in other columns.	Excessive carbon deposit or badly-seating valves—engine needs top-overhaul.
	Wrong type of sparking plugs fitted, overheating and causing pre-ignition.		Worn bearings, pistons or other mechanical faults.

STEERING FAULTS

Symptom
Heavy Steering

Probable Cause
Low pressures in front tyres.
Inadequate lubricant in steering unit and/or joints.
Incorrect steering adjustments.

Excessive Free Movement at Steering Wheel

Wear in steering linkage. The outer ball-joints are self-adjusting and if slackness develops they should be renewed.
Wear in steering rack-and-pinion assembly. Adjustment (by a dealer) may correct this. Otherwise fit a reconditioned assembly.
Steering mounting bolts slack.
Steering-column flexible coupling bolts loose.

Steering Wander
A tendency to wander and general lack of precision may be caused by slackness at any point in the steering gear (see above). Otherwise, check for faults in the next column.

Low or uneven tyre pressures. If the rear tyre pressures are too low, the car will "oversteer" and will be affected by side winds at speed.
Steering geometry incorrect. Have the geometry checked by a service station which possesses first-class modern equipment.
Distortion or damage to steering or suspension units. This may be caused by a minor collision and will be revealed by checks, carried out with precision equipment, against the measurements specified in the workshop manual. Normally a job for the expert.

Wheel Wobble or Steering Vibration at Speed

Unbalanced wheels and tyres will cause vibration, often at about 60–70 m.p.h. Have wheels and tyres checked both for static and dynamic balance.
Incorrect steering geometry. See "Steering Wander," above.
Slackness in steering gear. See "Excessive Free Movement at Steering Wheel," above.
Weak shock absorbers.

BRAKING SYSTEM FAULTS

Symptom
Excessive Pedal Travel

Probable Cause
Brakes require adjustment (see Chapter 9). If fault occurs only after prolonged or excessive use of brakes, it is caused by "brake fade." Normal braking will be restored when brakes cool down.

Brake Pedal Feels Spongy or Requires Pumping to Operate Brakes

Air in hydraulic system. Check level of fluid in reservoir, top-up if necessary and bleed brakes (see Chapter 9). Check for leaks throughout.
Main cup in master cylinder worn. Have components renewed by service station.
Excessive end-float on front-wheel hub bearings.

BRAKING SYSTEM FAULTS

Symptom	Probable Cause
Brakes Lack Power (See also "Excessive Pedal Travel," above)	Worn friction linings or pads, or oil or grease on linings or pads. Fit replacements (see Chapter 9). Scored or distorted brake drums or discs. Fit new drums or discs. Defective piston cups or seals in cylinders or callipers. Have new parts fitted throughout. Defective brake servo (when fitted).
Brakes Bind	Handbrake adjustment too tight or cable binding. Swollen piston or seal in brake cylinder or master cylinder. Compensating port in master cylinder obstructed by grit or swollen main cup. Master cylinder should be overhauled by an expert. Defective brake servo (when fitted).
Brakes Grab	Friction linings or pads contaminated with oil or grease. Sometimes the brakes may grab slightly after the car has stood overnight in damp weather. This is not a serious fault, if symptom disappears during normal running. Loose front-hub bearings. Distorted or badly scored drum or disc.
Brakes Pull to One Side	Unequal tyre pressures. Grease or oil on friction linings. Worn or glazed friction linings. Restriction in flexible brake hose or faulty operating cylinder in brake on opposite side to which steering pulls. Wear in front suspension or steering components.

GENERATOR AND CHARGING SYSTEM FAULTS

As a quick check on whether the battery is well charged and the cables and connections are in good condition, switch on the headlights and operate the starter. If the lights dim only slightly and the starter turns the engine at normal speed, it can be assumed that the battery and main wiring system are sound.

If the lights become very dim or go out when the starter is operated, check first for loose or dirty connections at the battery terminals, at the starter motor or solenoid-operated switch and at the connection between the battery earthing cable and the bodywork. A rusty or corroded contact here is often overlooked. If these checks are satisfactory, have the battery tested by a service station which possesses the correct equipment.

These preliminary checks should always be made before attempting to diagnose any of the faults listed below.

Symptom	*Probable Cause*

**Battery Charge
Consistently Low**

A low state of charge may be due simply to the drain caused by frequent starting, short journeys and night driving, when the output from the alternator is often insufficient to meet the current drawn from the battery. During the winter months it may be necessary to use a trickle charger regularly in such circumstances. But first check for the faults in the next column.

Defective battery. Sulphated plates will not accept a full charge. Buckled plates or an accumulation of sediment will cause internal leakage of current. Have battery checked by an expert.

Loose alternator driving belt. Check tension of belt and adjust if necessary.

Insufficient output from generator. Have output tested by service station. New brushes may be required or a replacement generator may be needed.

Faulty generator regulator. A moving-coil voltmeter is needed when checking and adjusting the regulator. Again a job for the expert.

Loose connections or a broken wire in charging circuit.

**Battery Consistently
Overcharged**

This fault is indicated by the need for frequent topping-up of the battery with distilled water.

Regulator set to give too high a charging rate. Have setting checked by a service station.

13 Saving money on repairs

MAJOR repairs are not normally within the scope of the average owner, who is often forced to work under somewhat cramped conditions. There is also the unfortunate fact that the design of modern cars calls for the use of a fairly extensive range of special tools if ambitious work is undertaken, and the expense of these will not be justified if only occasional jobs are to be done. Sometimes it is possible to do without the recommended service tool, but makeshift methods seldom pay in the long run.

It is these factors which have resulted in the widespread adoption nowadays of the reconditioned-unit exchange scheme, under which factory-rebuilt parts can be obtained in exchange for the worn or faulty units. The advantage of this arrangement, of course, is that the unit carries the manufacturer's guarantee and that repair is simply a matter of removing the old part and installing the new one.

There is, however, another side to the picture. Some garages are rather too inclined to take the easy way out and to fit a reconditioned replacement when the faulty unit could be repaired at a much lower cost. It is not surprising, therefore, that many practical owners prefer to do as much of the actual repair work as possible, thus saving not only high labour charges, but also the cost of parts which are still serviceable. An example is a partial engine overhaul, described later in this chapter.

When this has been said, one must still draw a line somewhere. For example, gearbox (or automatic transmission) and rear axle overhauls are beyond the scope of the owner, and this also applies to some other units. Experience has shown that unless these jobs are done under workshop conditions, using special tools and gauges when necessary, further trouble is almost inevitable.

Without the right tools, some jobs cannot be done at all, or at best only in a botched-up way that will never prove satisfactory. Owners are not alone, of course, in using makeshift methods. Only too often one sees garage mechanics doing a job which calls for precision workmanship in a horrifyingly casual manner. It *may* be possible to hire the tools from a dealer, against a deposit to cover their value, especially if you are already a good customer of the garage.

When tackling the overhauls described later in this chapter, a workshop manual is also virtually essential. Not only is it necessary to follow the correct procedure during dismantling and reassembly, but the fits and clearances laid down in the manual must be strictly adhered to.

Engine Overhauls. If an engine has covered a very high mileage, a partial overhaul may not restore full power. Instead, it may be necessary to rebore the cylinders and to fit oversize pistons, although rebores are not often necessary nowadays. The crankshaft journals, however, may have to be reground to take undersize connecting-rod and main-bearing shells, and the timing chain and sprockets, and possibly also the oil pump and the starter ring gear, may have to be renewed. Undoubtedly the most satisfactory (and often the cheapest) course in such cases is to fit a re-conditioned engine, which can be obtained under the service-exchange scheme operated by dealers.

In spite of what has just been said, however, an owner is often persuaded to have a new engine fitted when heavy oil consumption, piston-slap and low oil pressure could have been cured for an expenditure of quite a small sum (seldom exceedine £15-£20), provided that the owner was able to carry out the necessary dismantling and assembly, the worn components being sent to a specialist firm for reconditioning or replacement. If the engine has not covered more than about 40,000 miles, it is worth giving careful consideration to this alternative.

One firm that has made a special study of the effectiveness of recondi-tioning modern engines in this way is G.M.A. Reconsets Ltd., Dunston Rd., Chesterfield, Derbyshire. As a result of their experience, they supply a standard reconditioning kit which includes new pistons, fitted with special oil-control rings (normally rendering reboring unnecessary), a piston-ring compressor, a set of connecting-rod bearing shells, new exhaust valves, a complete set of valve springs, a valve-grinding tool, a timing chain, a complete set of gaskets, gasket cement, an oil filter and graphite assembly compound.

It is not always realized, when trying to asses whether a partial overhaul will be satisfactory, that the condition of the crankshaft is likely to be more important that the amount of wear on the cylinder bores. This is because excessive clearances in the connecting-rod bearings can result in more oil reaching the cylinder walls than can be controlled even by new pistons and special oil-control rings.

If the engine has covered more than 40,000 miles, therefore, it would be as well to enlist the aid of someone who can measure the crankpins with a micrometer. If the wear exceeds 0·001 in., it is advisable to have the crankshaft re-ground. Even half a "thou" of wear can often cause an appreciable increase in oil consumption.

Fitting new connecting-rod bearing shells is usually all that is required, however, when a partial overhaul is undertaken at between 30,000–40,000 miles, In any event, the shells should be replaced as a matter of routine at this mileage.

The bearings are of the thin-shell type which can be installed without the need for skilled fitting. No shims are used and the caps should on no account be filed or rubbed down to take up excessive clearance. Provided that the crankpins are not scored or badly worn, the installation of new bearing shells will give the correct running clearance and restore normal oil pressure.

It must be assumed, of course, that if you are prepared to tackle a partial or a major engine overhaul, you will have had some experience of engine dismantling, fitting and assembly, or will be able to rely on the guidance of an experienced mechanic. The do-it-yourself owner can also learn a lot of the essential "know-how" (which is not necessarily included in a workshop manual, concerned chiefly with dismantling, reassembly and adjustments), from practical handbooks such as *Automobile Workshop Practice*, which is published in Pitman's Automobile Maintenance Series.

Clutch Overhauls. Fitting a reconditioned clutch assembly should be within the scope of a practical owner but renewal of the clutch pilot bearing in the crankshaft flange calls for the use of a special tool and should be left to a Vauxhall dealer. To service the clutch, it is necessary to remove the gearbox and clutch-housing assembly. The car must, of course, be on axle stands or over a pit.

As it is possible to damage the clutch during removal or assembly, the safest plan is to work strictly to the detailed instructions in the workshop manual, which cannot be reproduced in the space available in this short chapter.

The Steering Gear. What has been said about clutch repairs applies also to overhauls of the steering gear rack-and-pinion unit. An owner can renew the ball joints on the outer ends of the track rods, but dismantling and reassembly of the rack-and-pinion unit is definitely a job for a dealer, as special gauges are needed to adjust the gear and apply the correct preload to the pinion and inner ball joints.

The Front Suspension. The front suspension is a fairly simple layout and no great difficulty should be experienced in renewing the various parts, provided that some means of holding the springs compressed can be devised. The safest plan is to use a pair of special tools, Part No. P5045, to avoid any risk of a makeshift restrainer failing at a critical moment during dismantling or reassembly. If a spring suddenly expands with considerable force, it could cause serious injury to anyone working on the suspension.

The Rear Suspension. The rear suspension, again, should not present many difficulties to an experienced owner but special tools are needed to remove and refit the bushes in the suspension links, and the rubber insulator assembly at the top of the spring, so it would be unwise to begin work without consulting your local dealer.

Index